2015

Mekhitar Garabedian

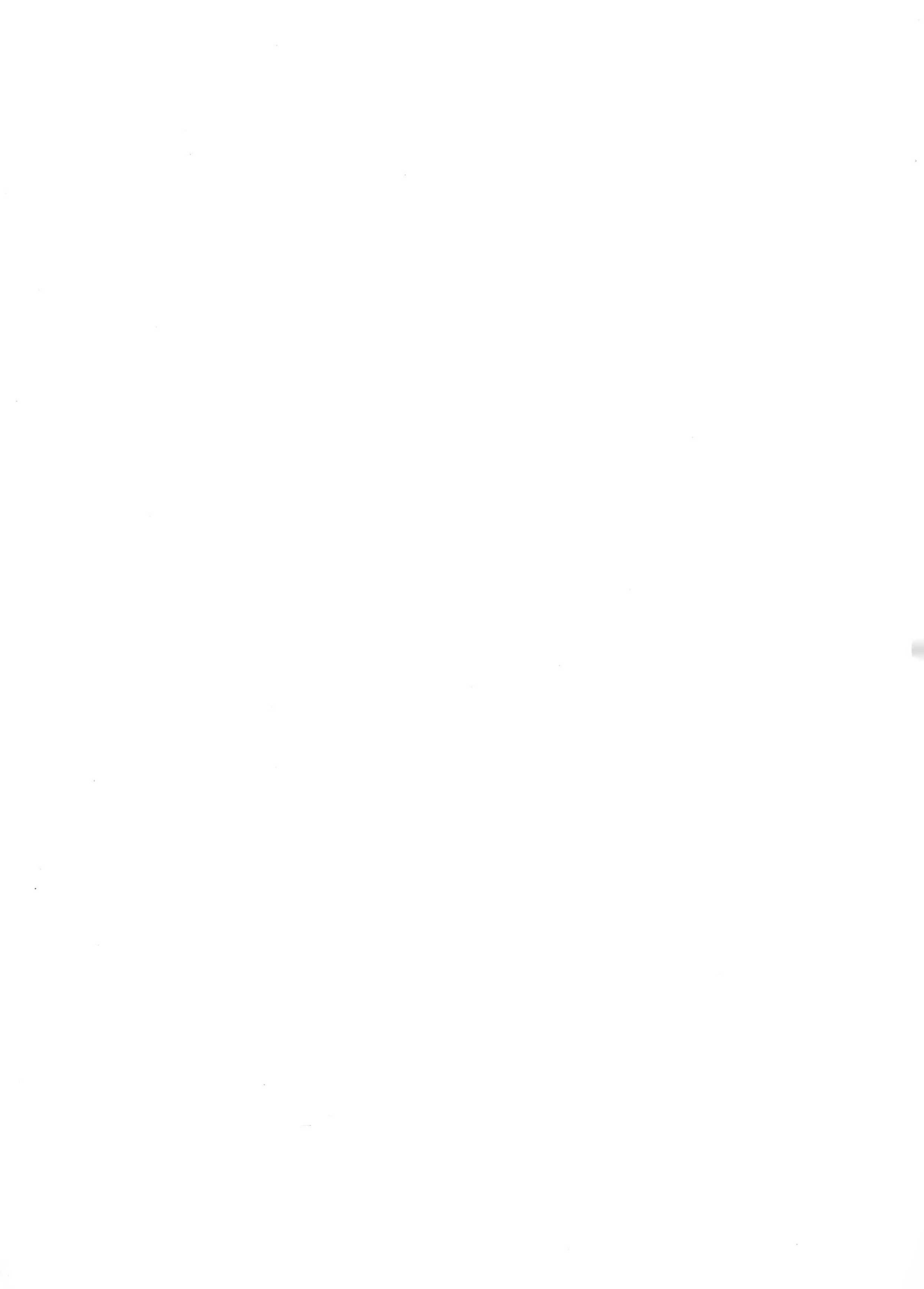

TABLE

02.08.2012
16.01.2012
24.05.2012
17.07.2012
15.11.2012
18.07.2013
04.04.2014
07.04.2014
19.04.2014
02.05.2014
16.06.2014
01.07.2014
07.07.2014
09.08.2014
11.08.2014
16.08.2014
21.08.2014
28.08.2014
02.09.2014
09.09.2014
11.09.2014
03.10.2014
06.10.2014
08.10.2014
09.10.2014
10.10.2014
11.10.2014
13.10.2014
17.10.2014
24.10.2014
26.10.2014
01.11.2014
05.11.2014
08.11.2014

12.11.2014
14.11.2014
13.11.2014
15.11.2014
27.11.2014
29.11.2014
05.12.2014
10.12.2014
12.12.2014
11.01.2015
04.02.2015
06.02.2015
12.02.2015
13.02.2015
23.02.2015
26.02.2015
27.02.2015
28.02.2015
02.03.2015
03.03.2015
09.03.2015
14.03.2015
16.03.2015
22.03.2015
25.03.2015
28.03.2015
30.03.2015
04.04.2015
07.04.2015
09.04.2015
10.04.2015
13.04.2015
14.04.2015
20.04.2015

GENTBRUGGE (KITCHEN)

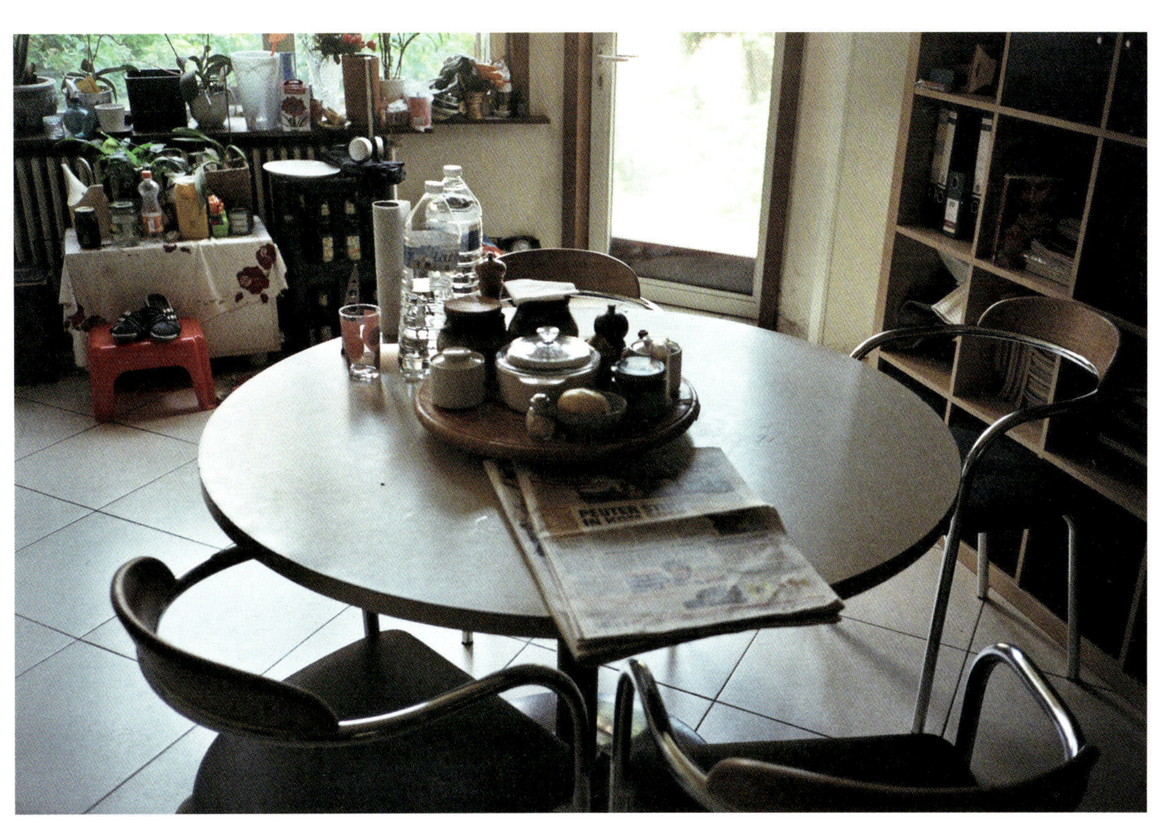

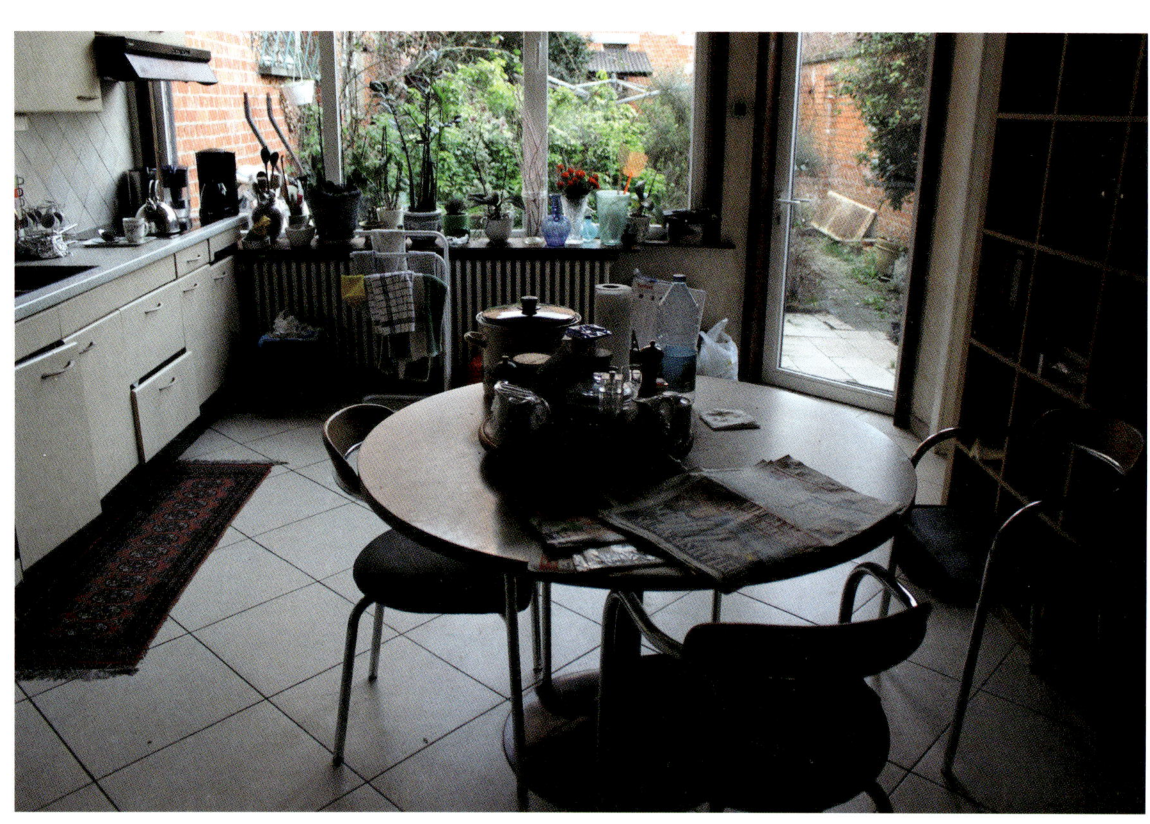

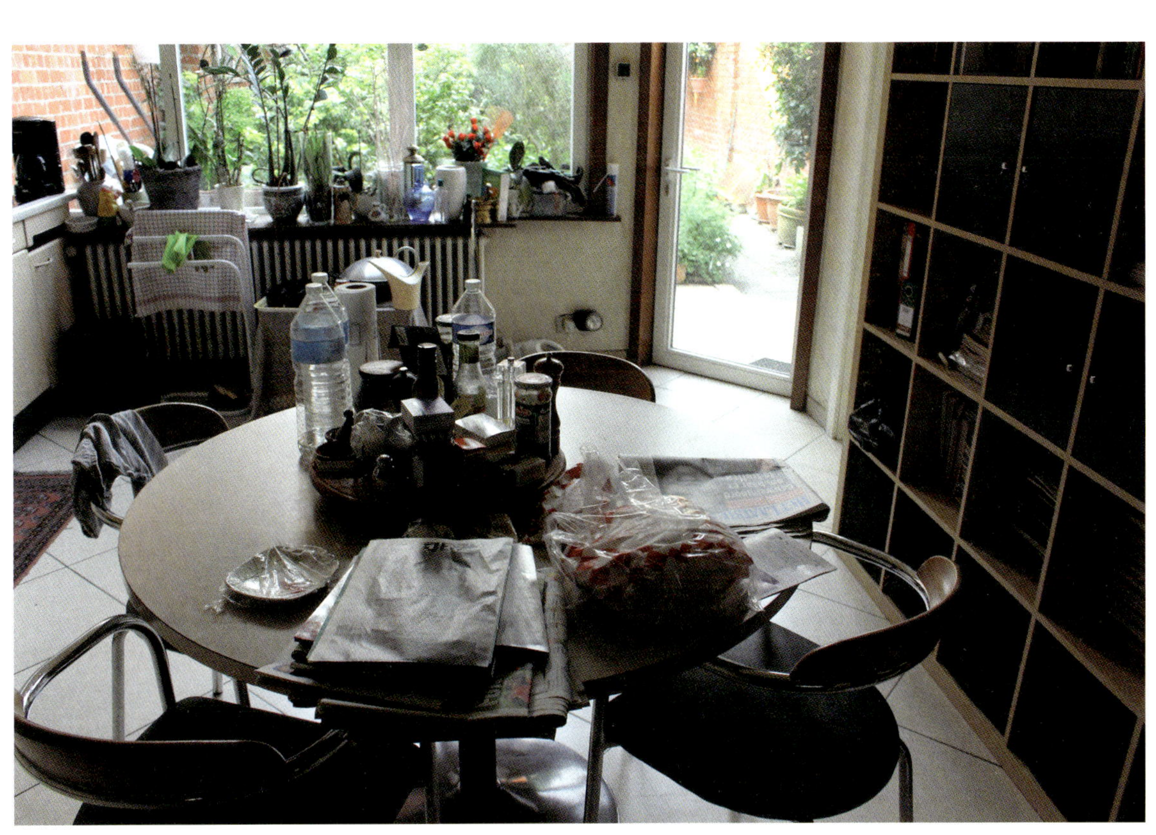

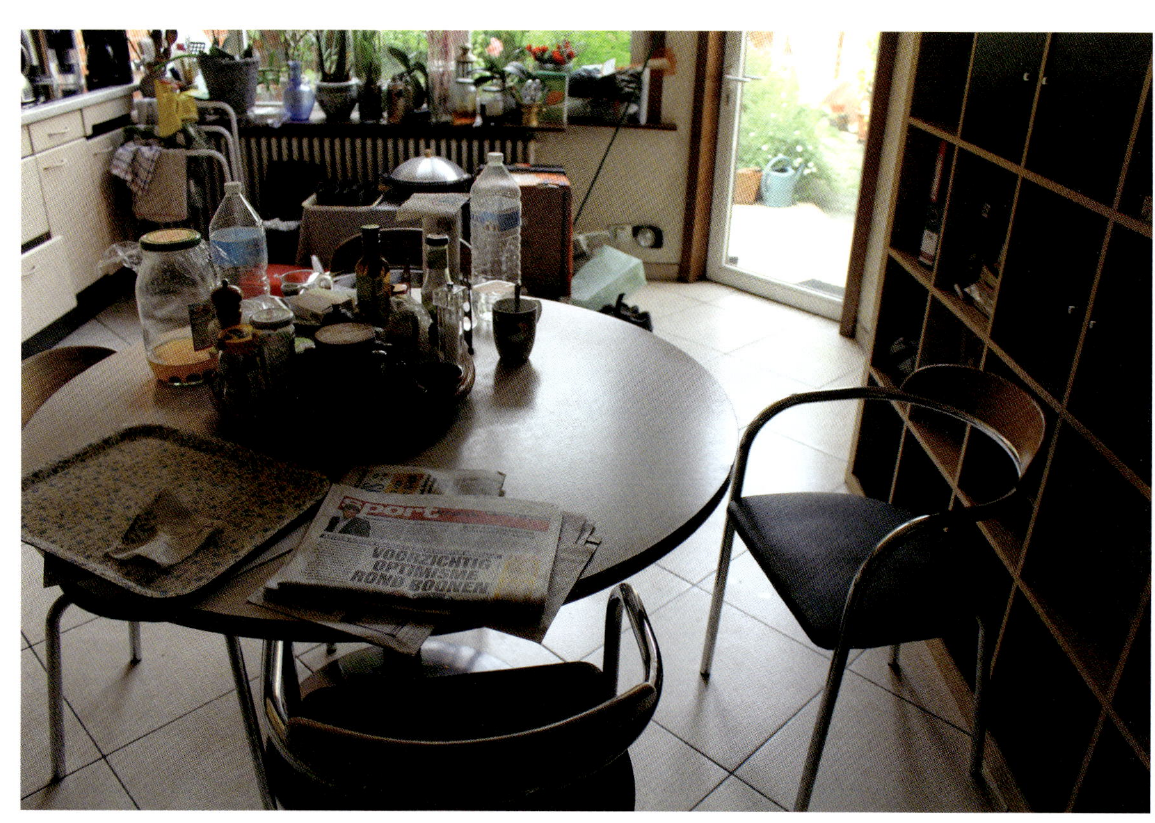
sport
VOORZICHTIG
OPTIMISME
ROND BOONEN

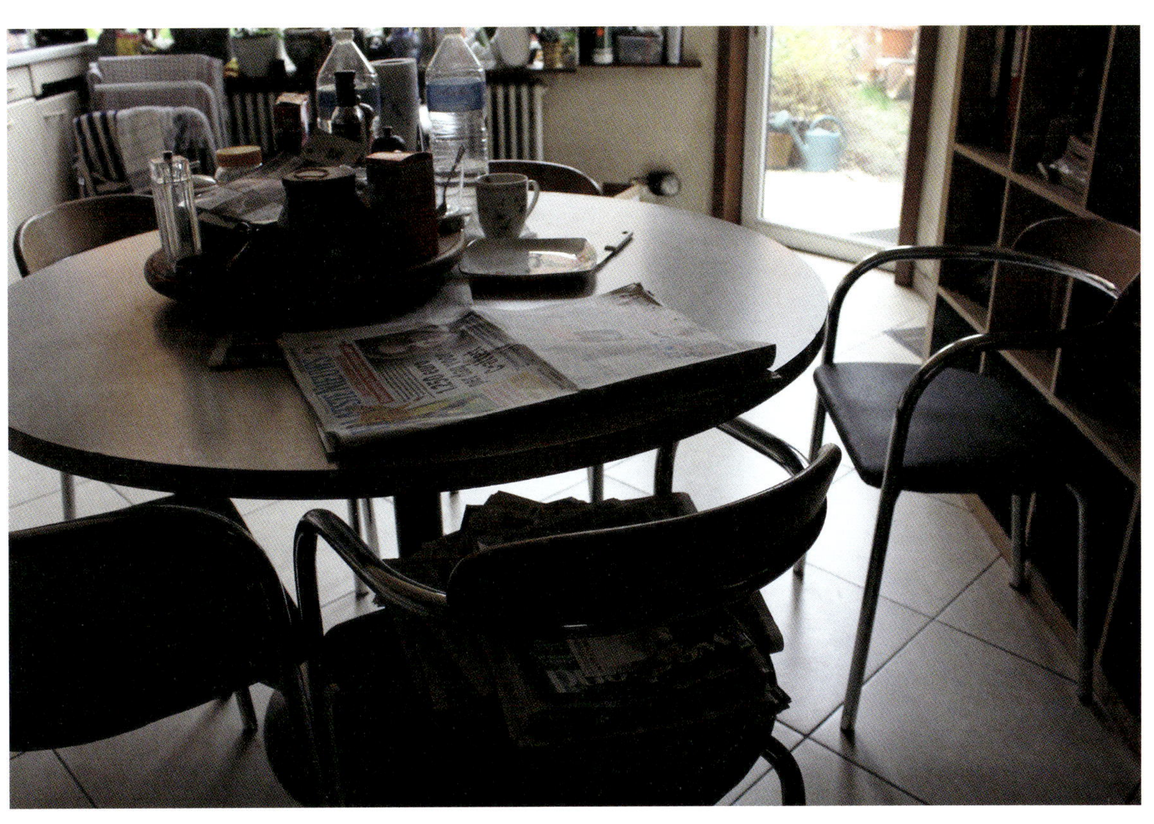

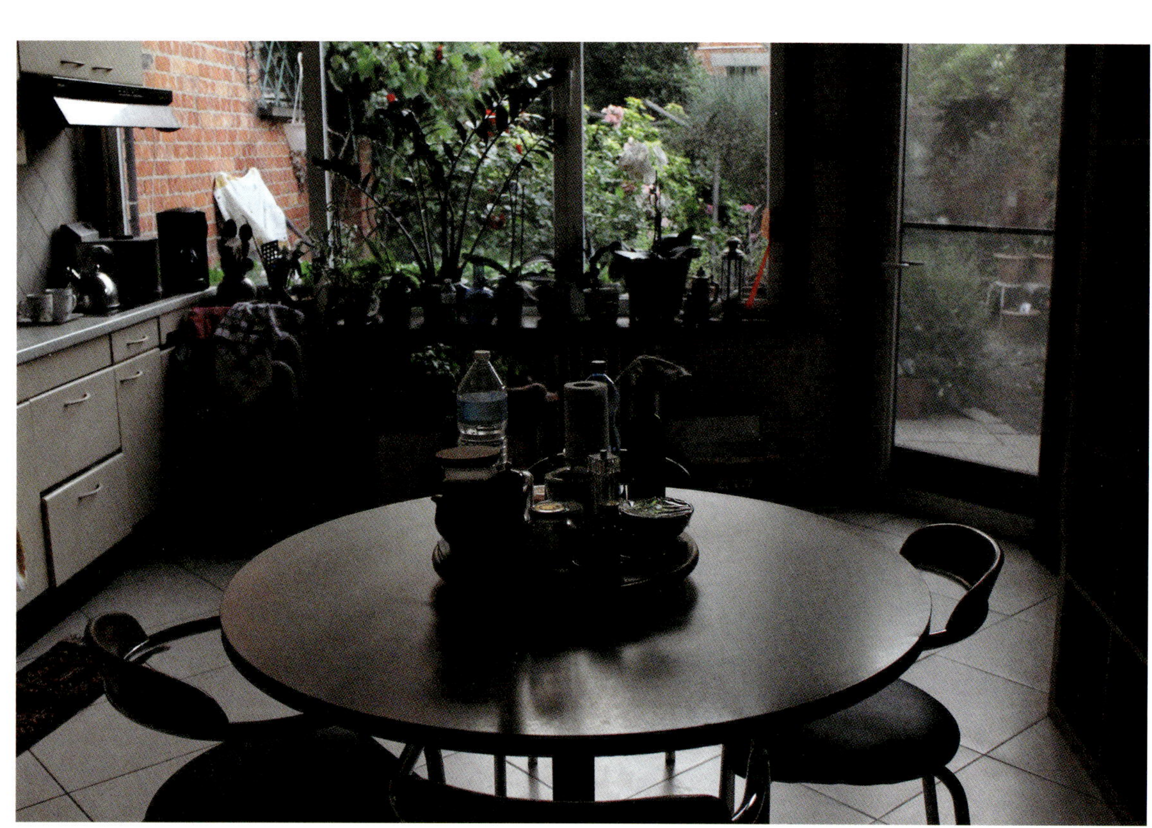

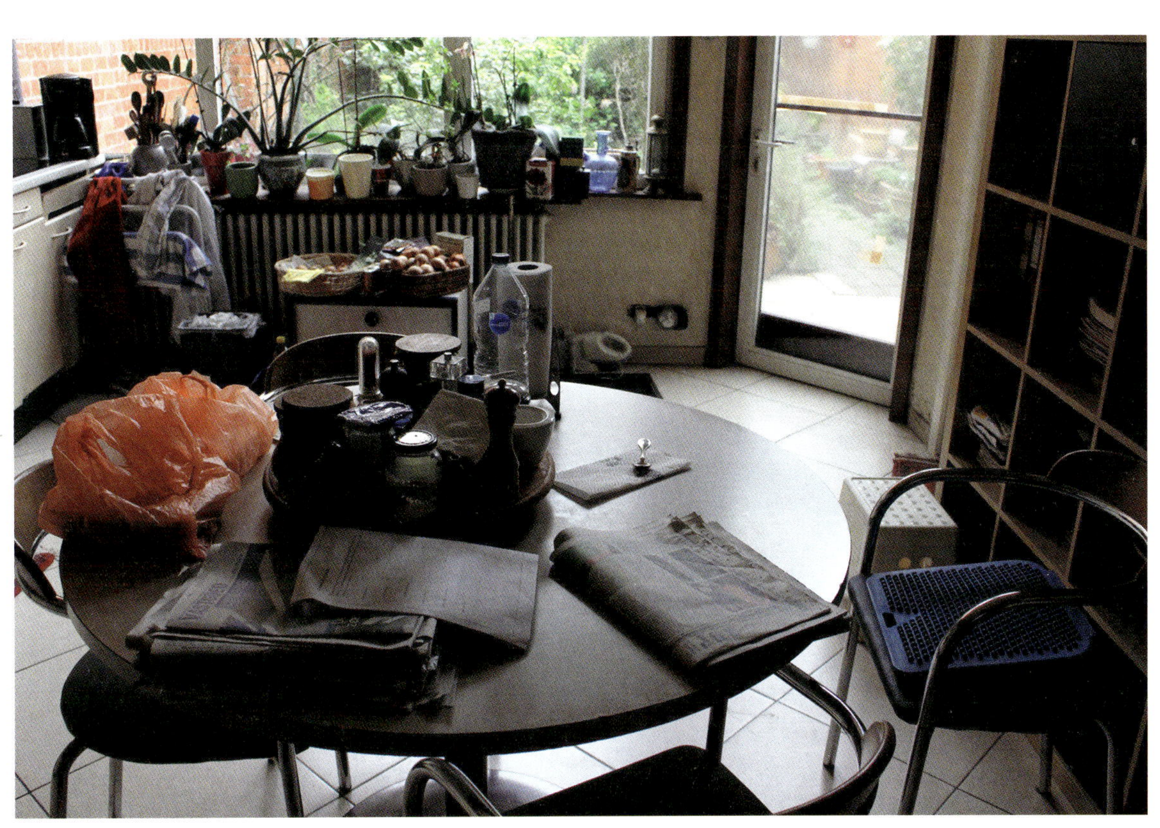

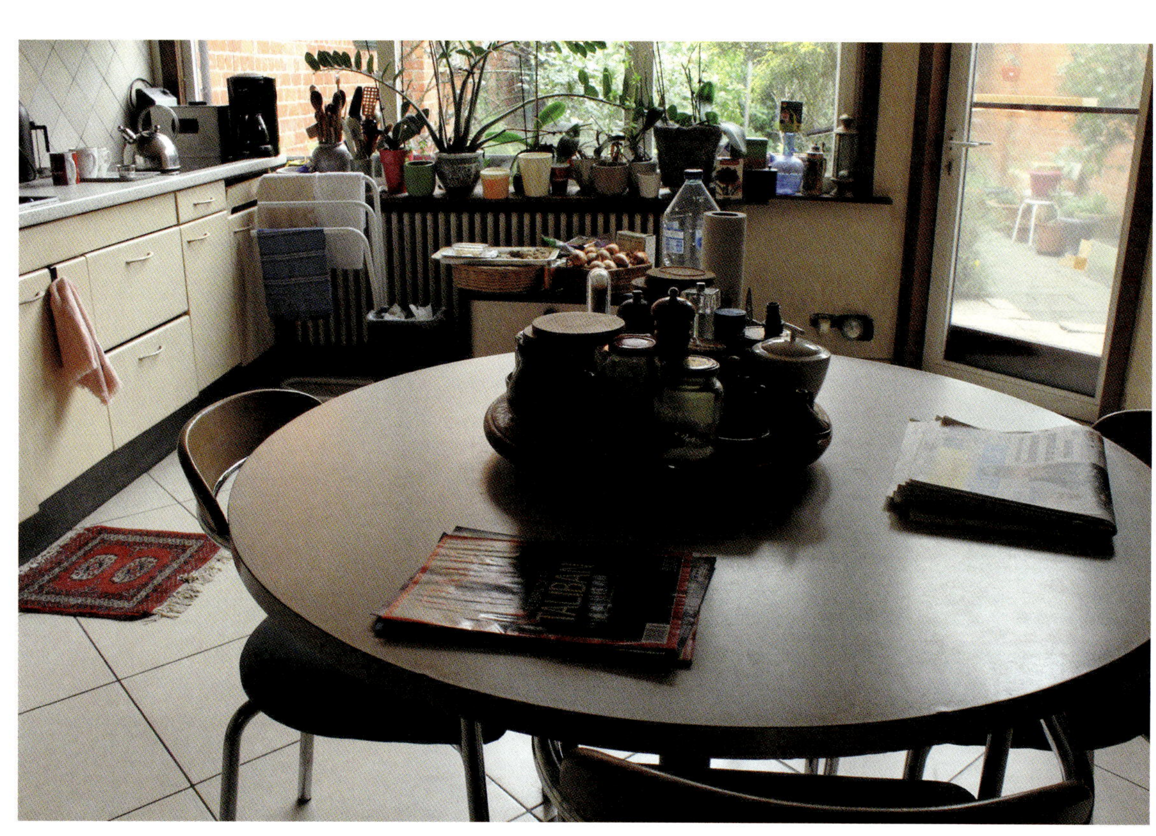

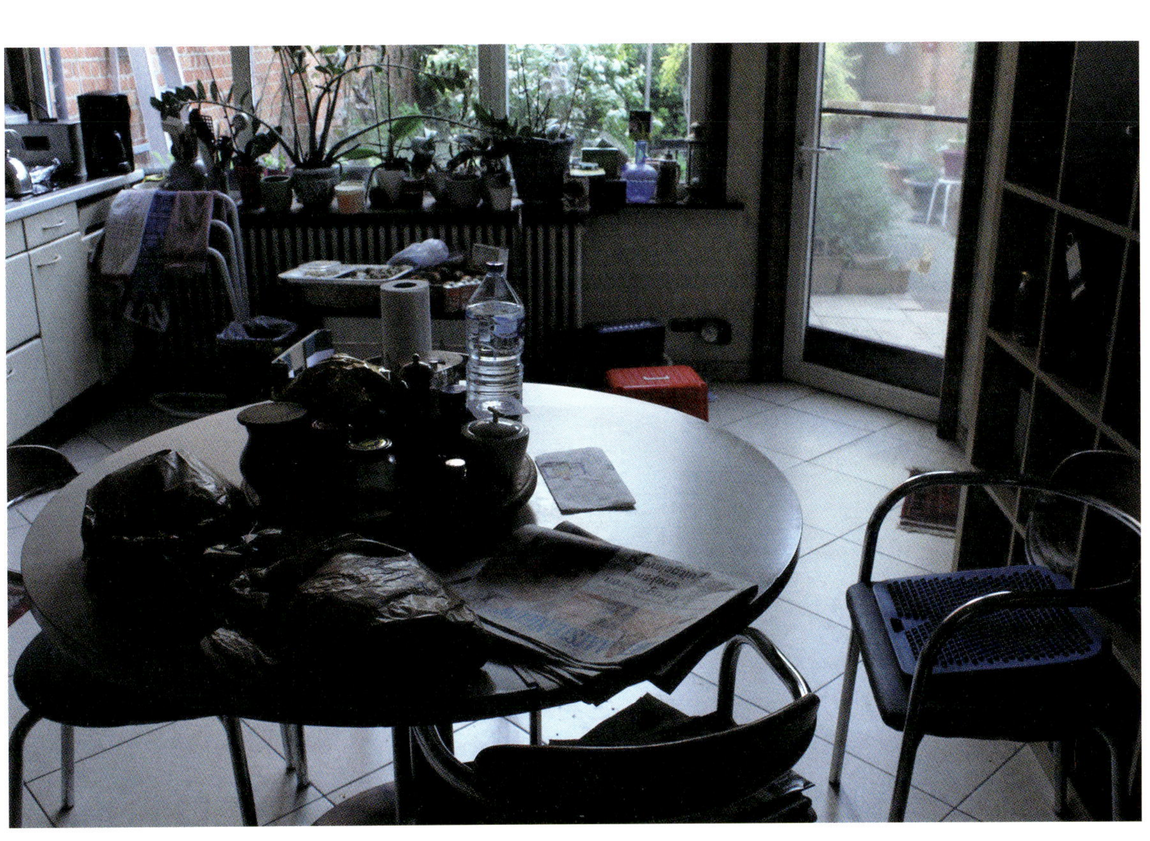

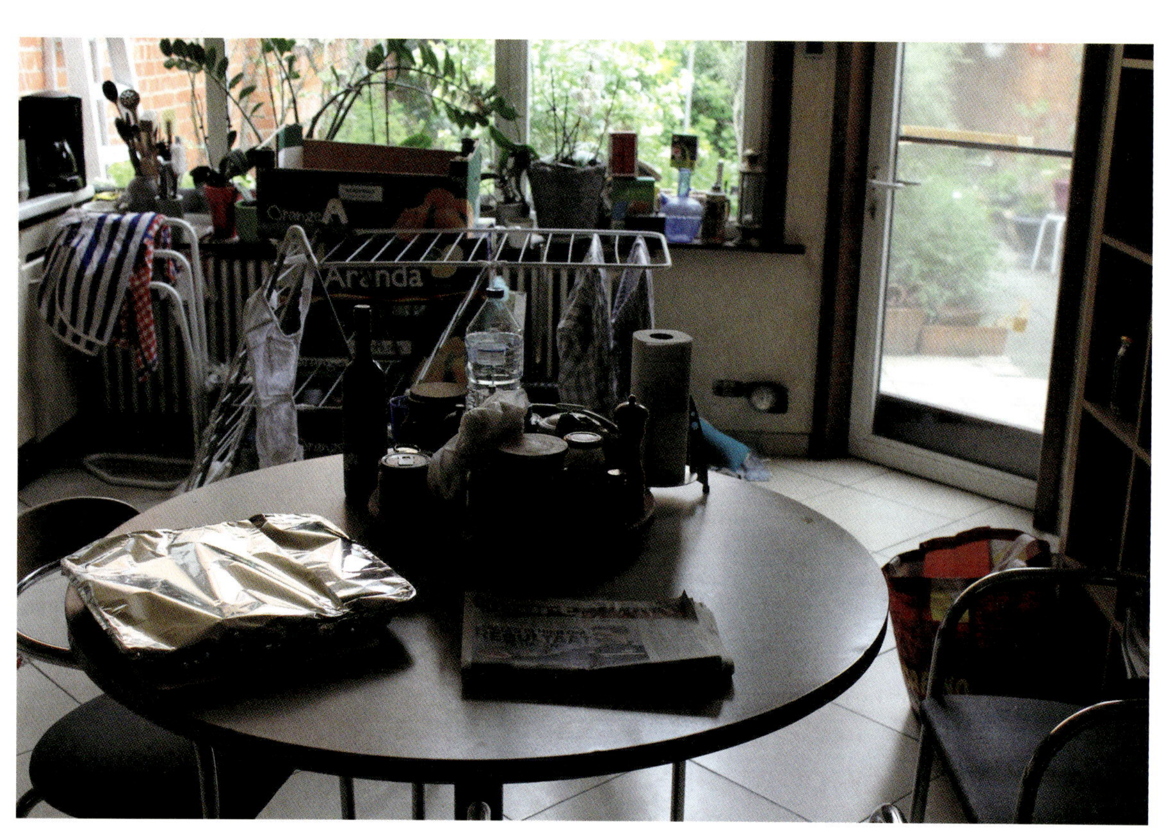

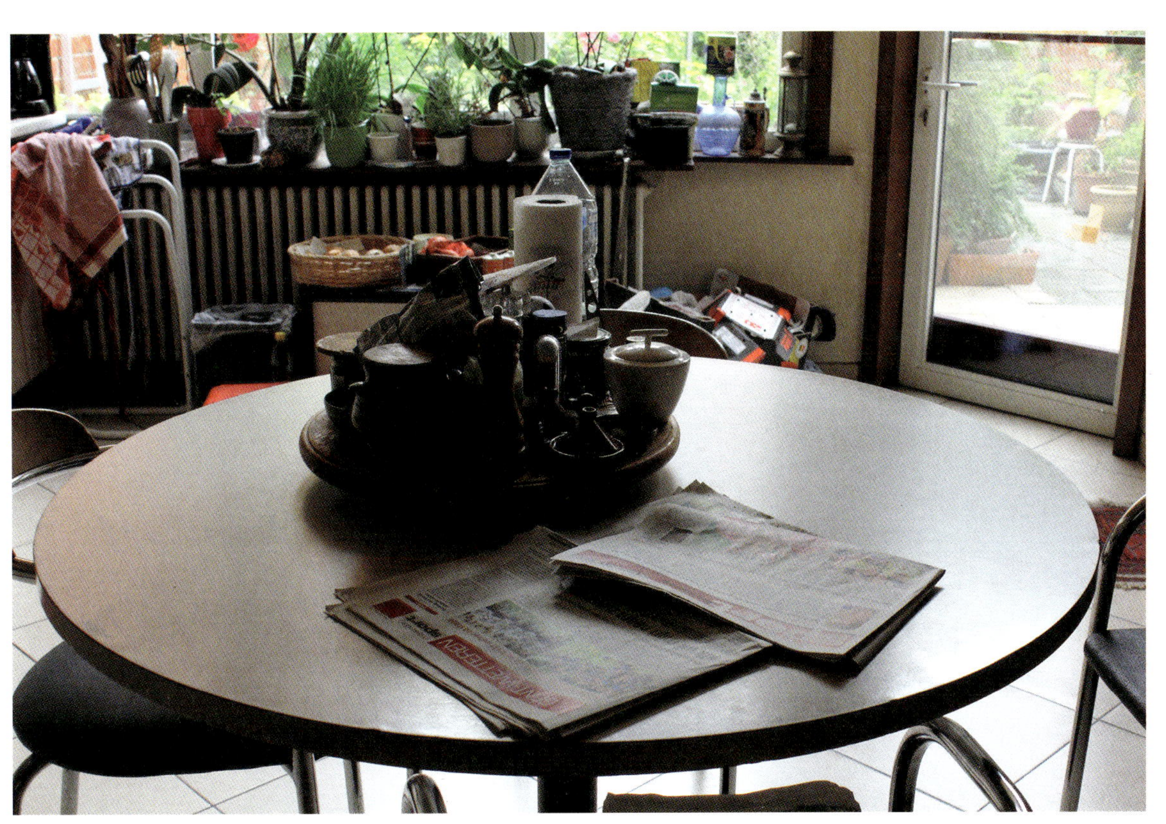

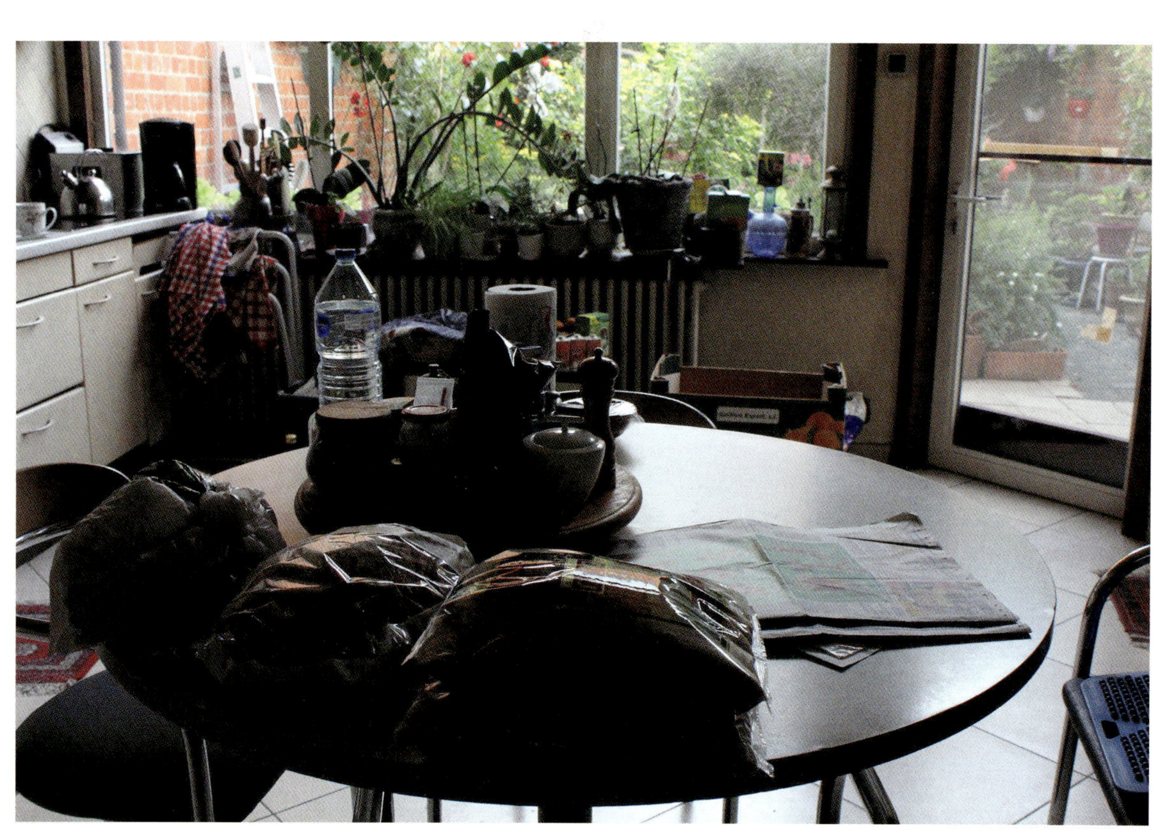

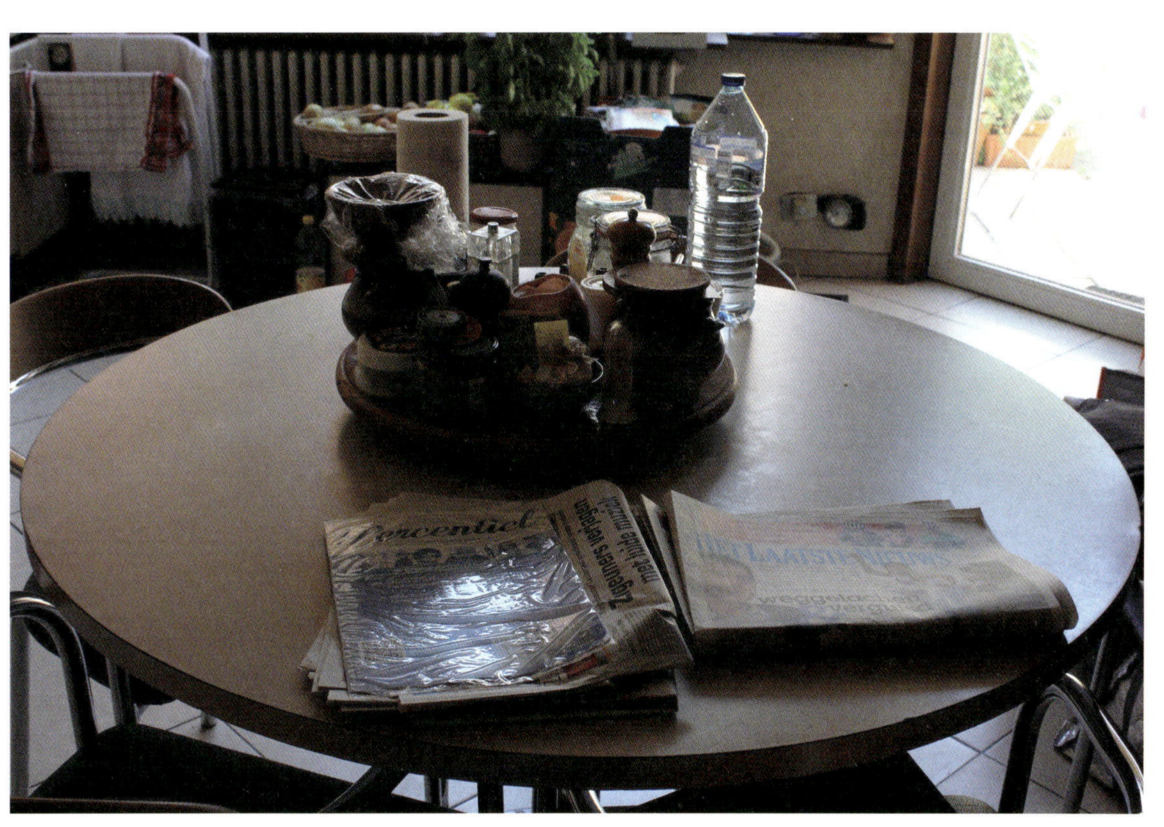

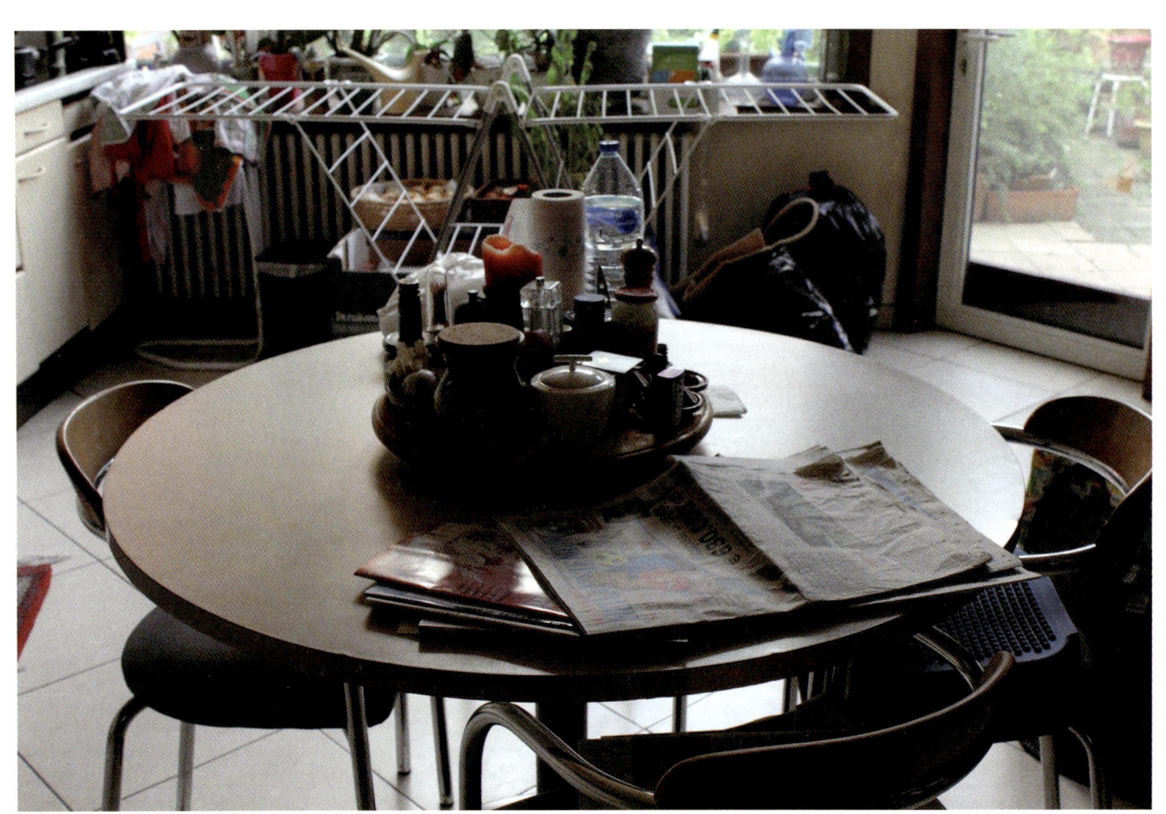

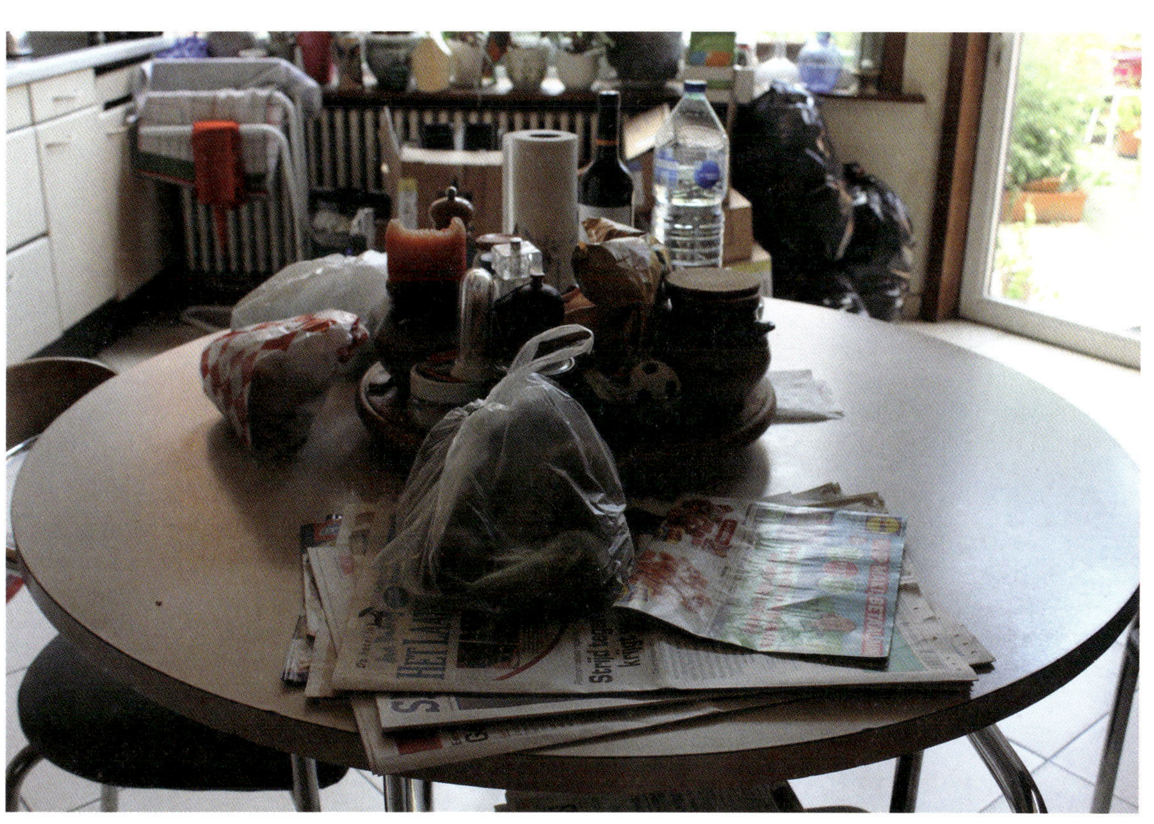

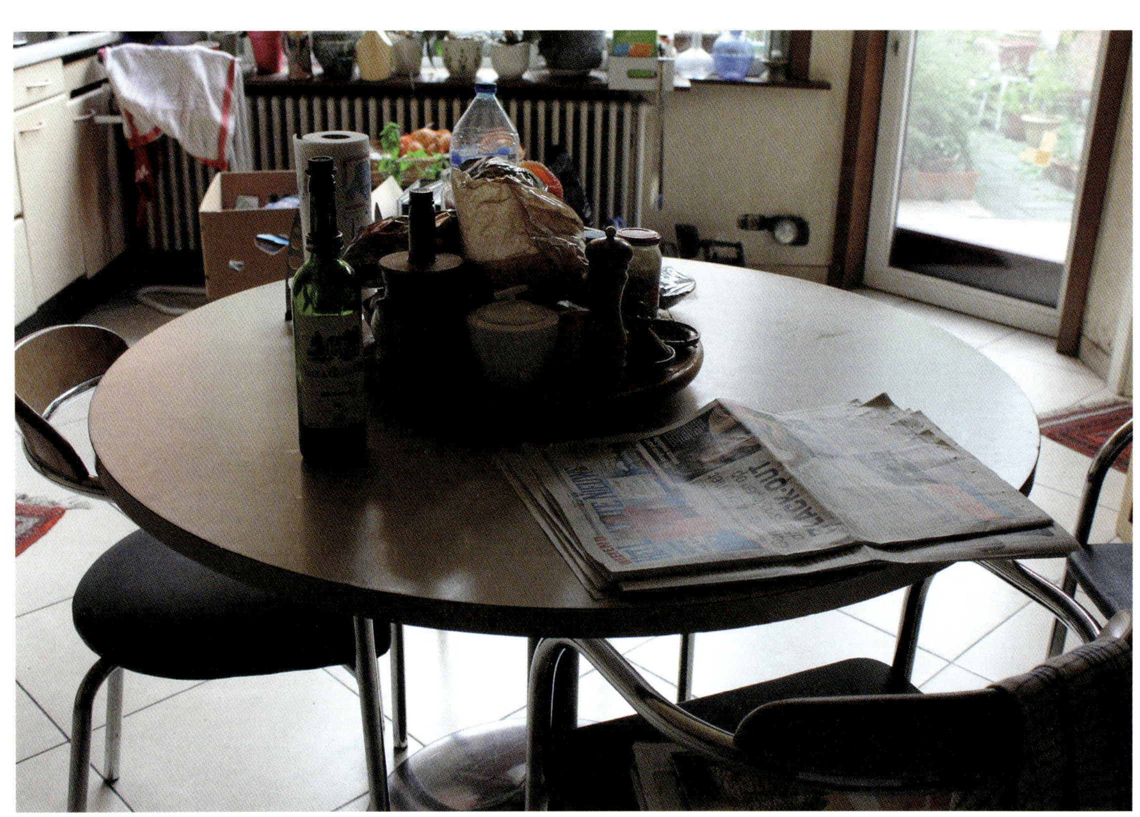

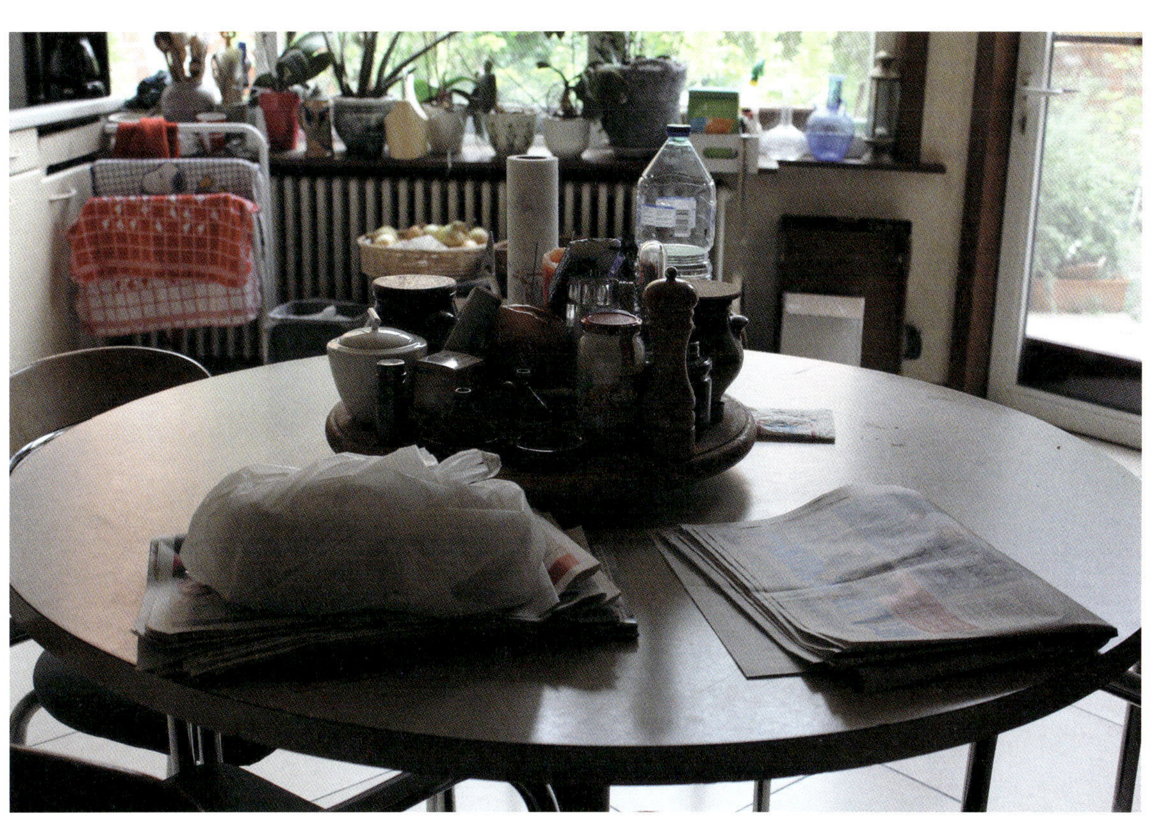

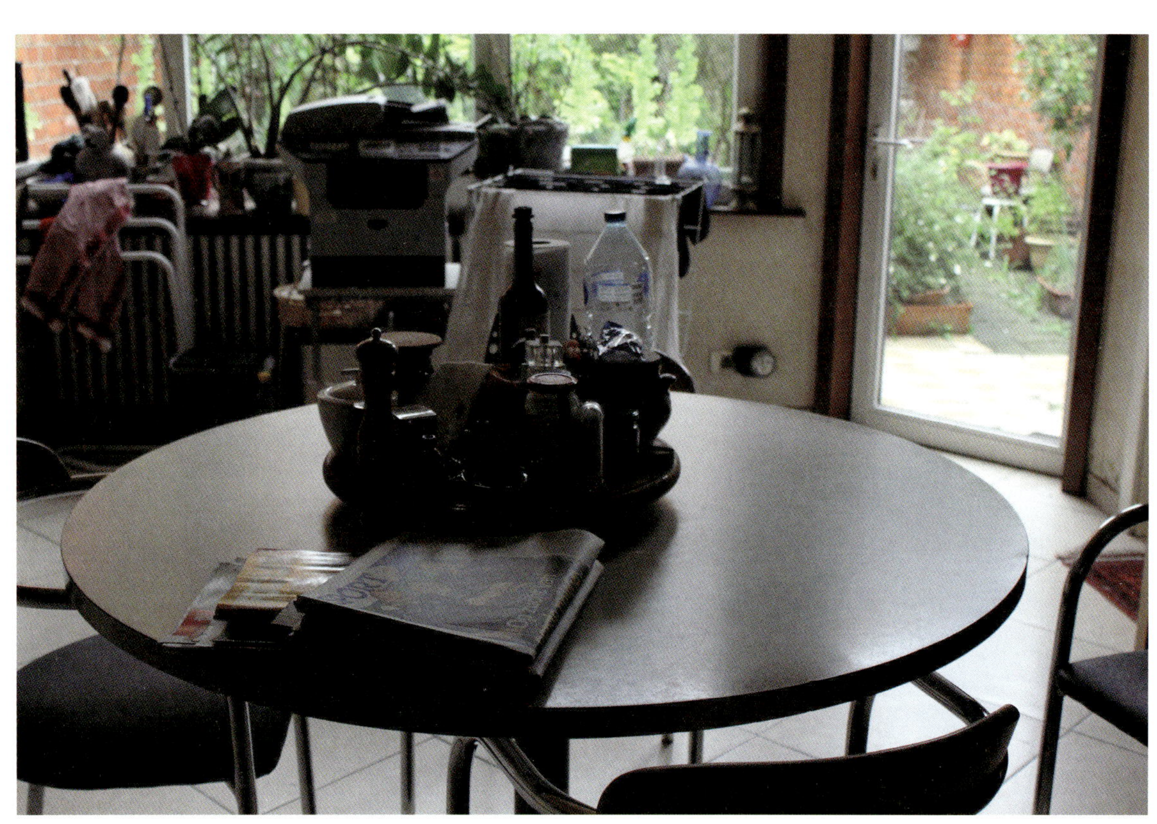

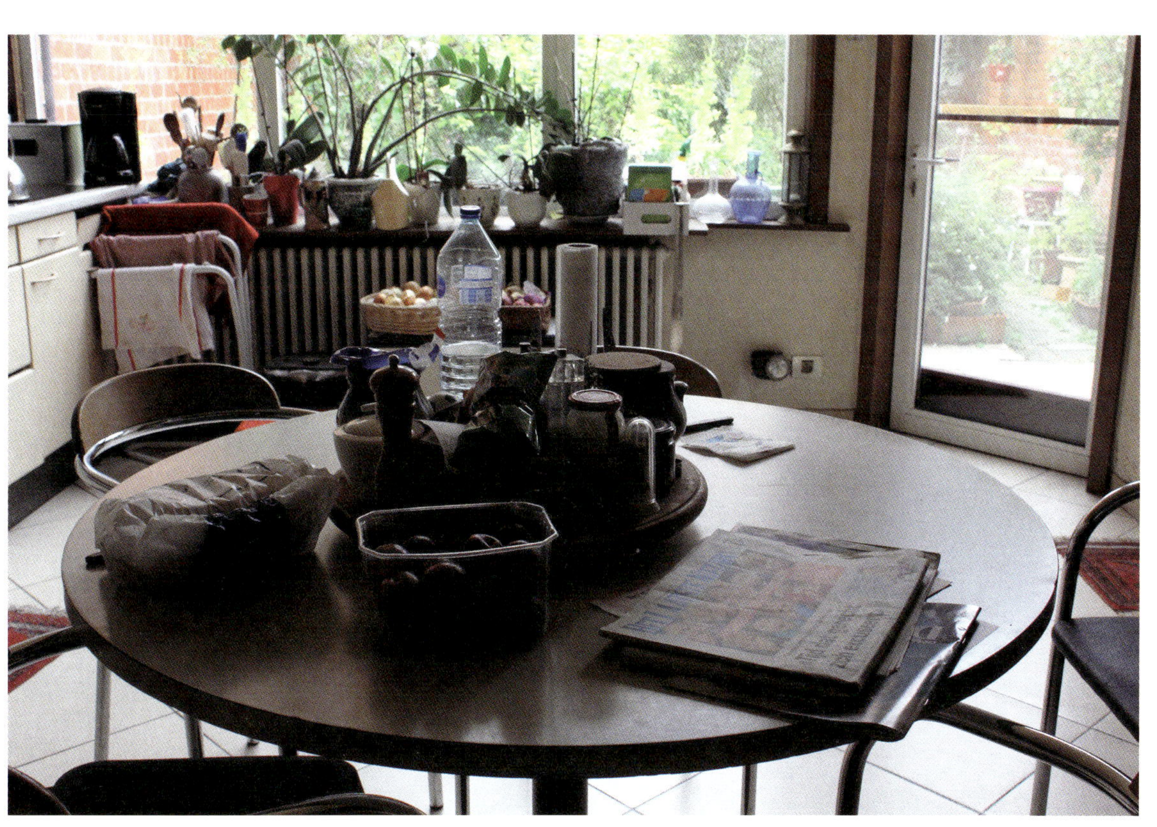

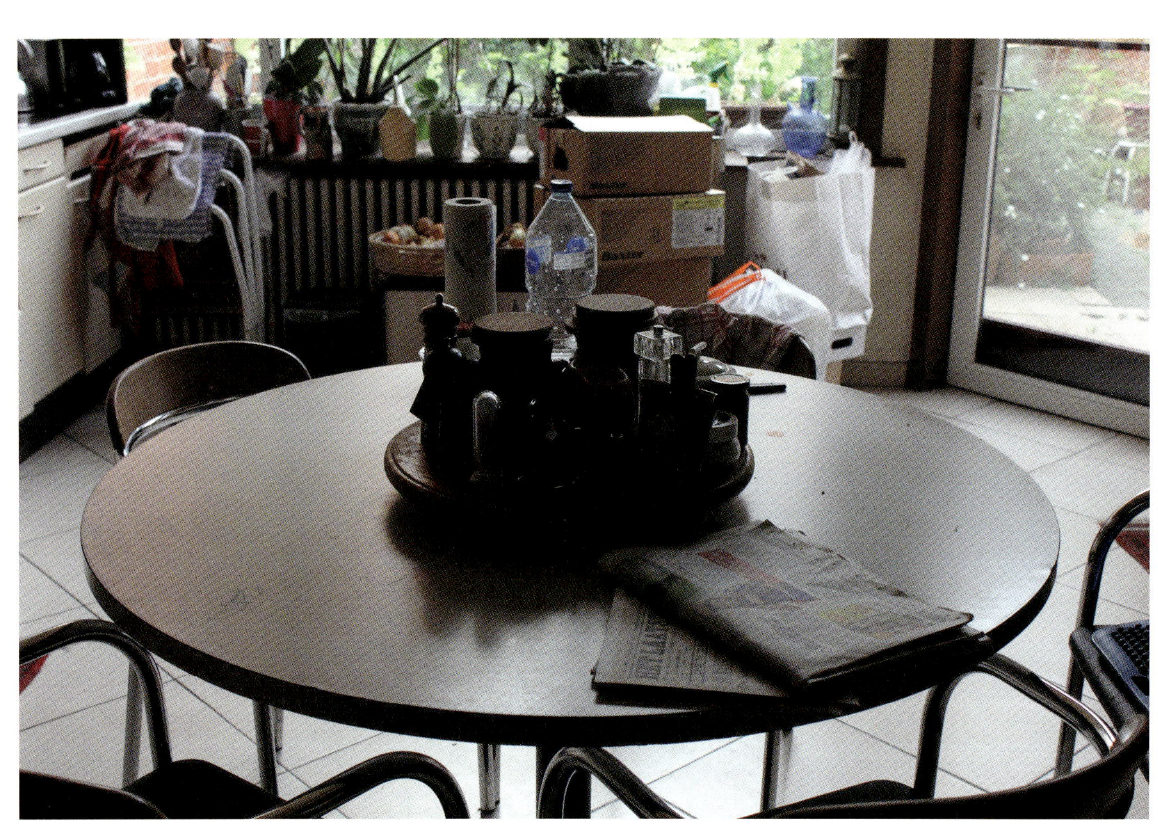

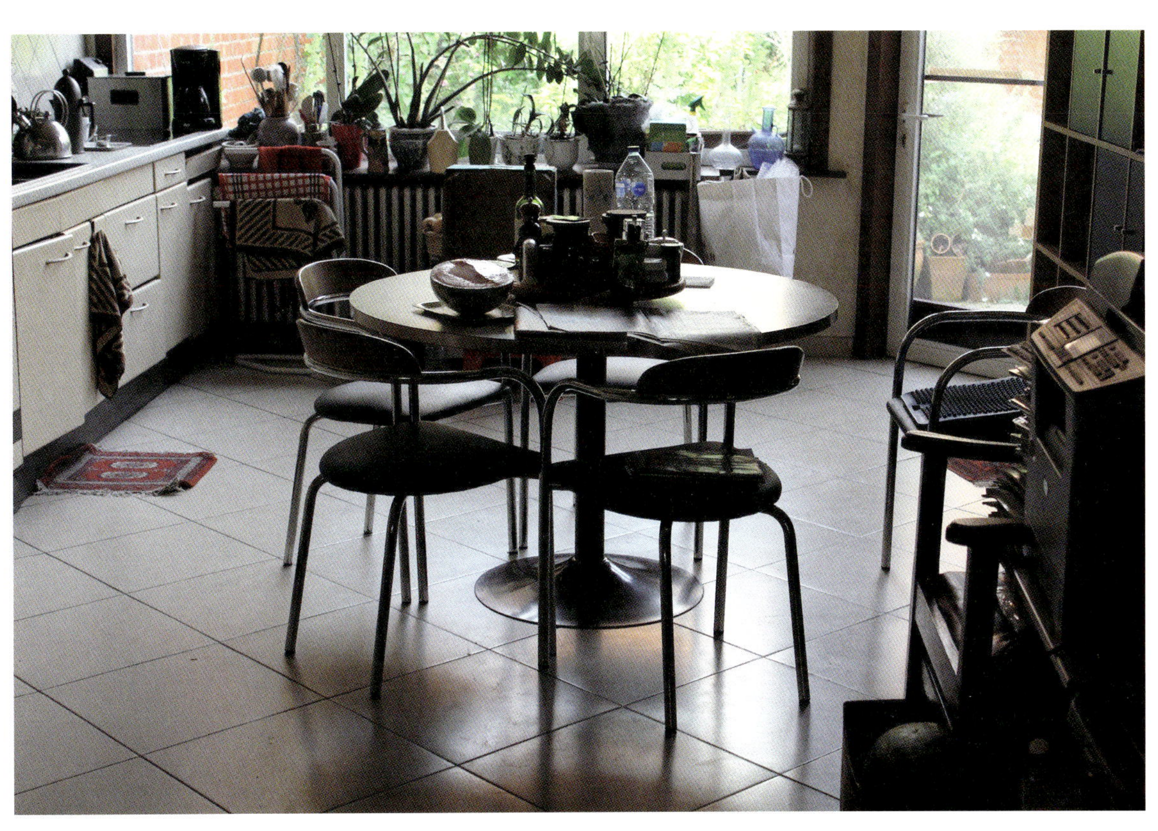

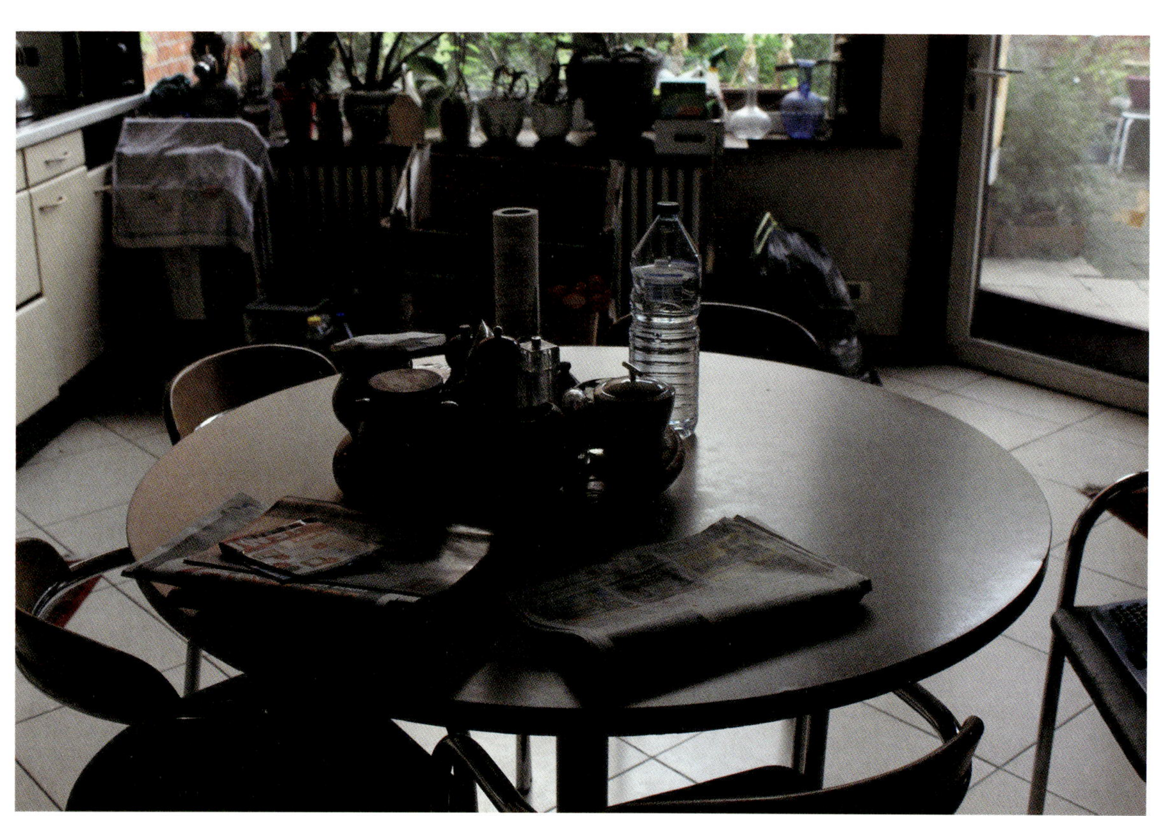

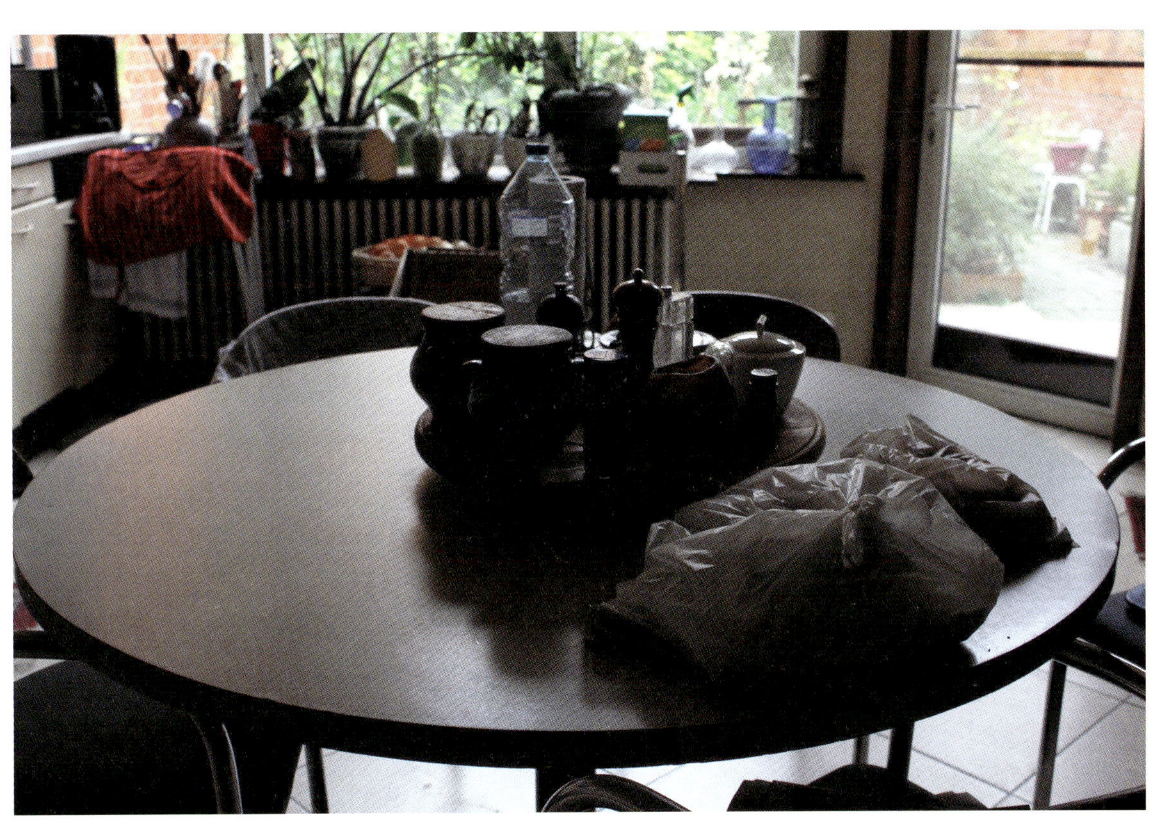

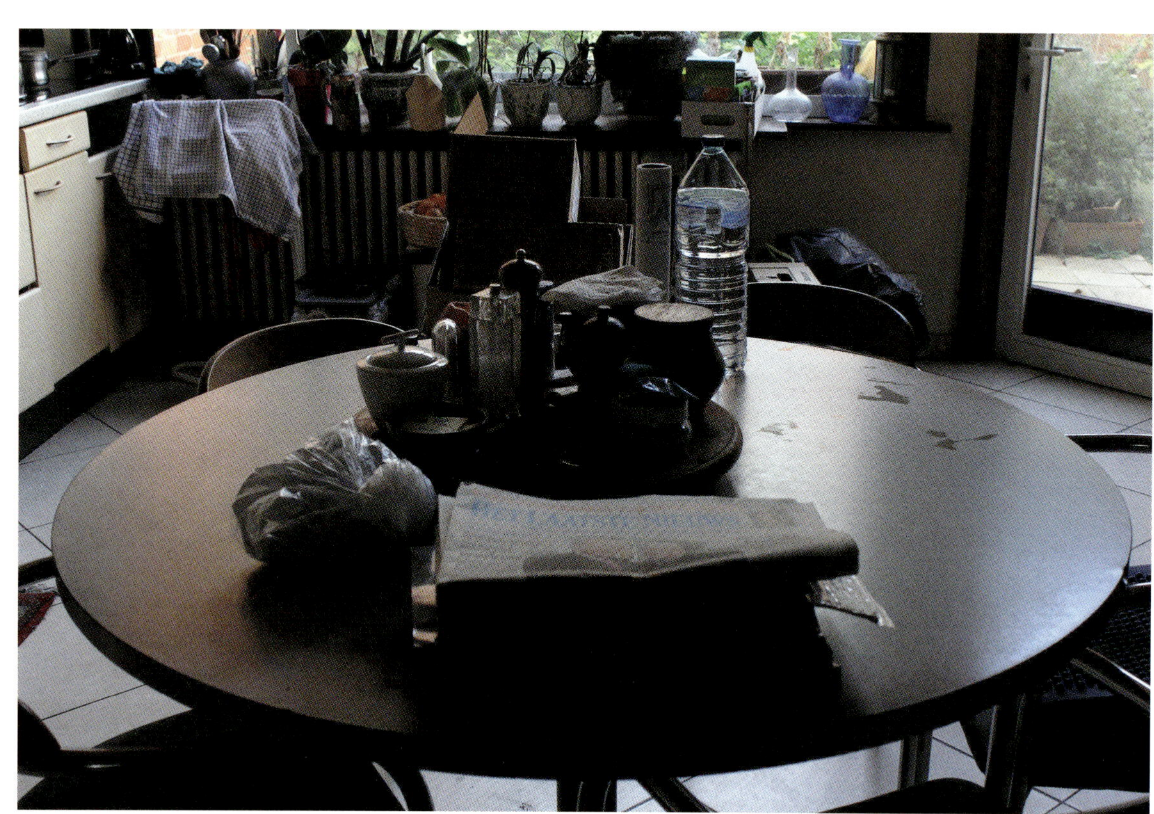

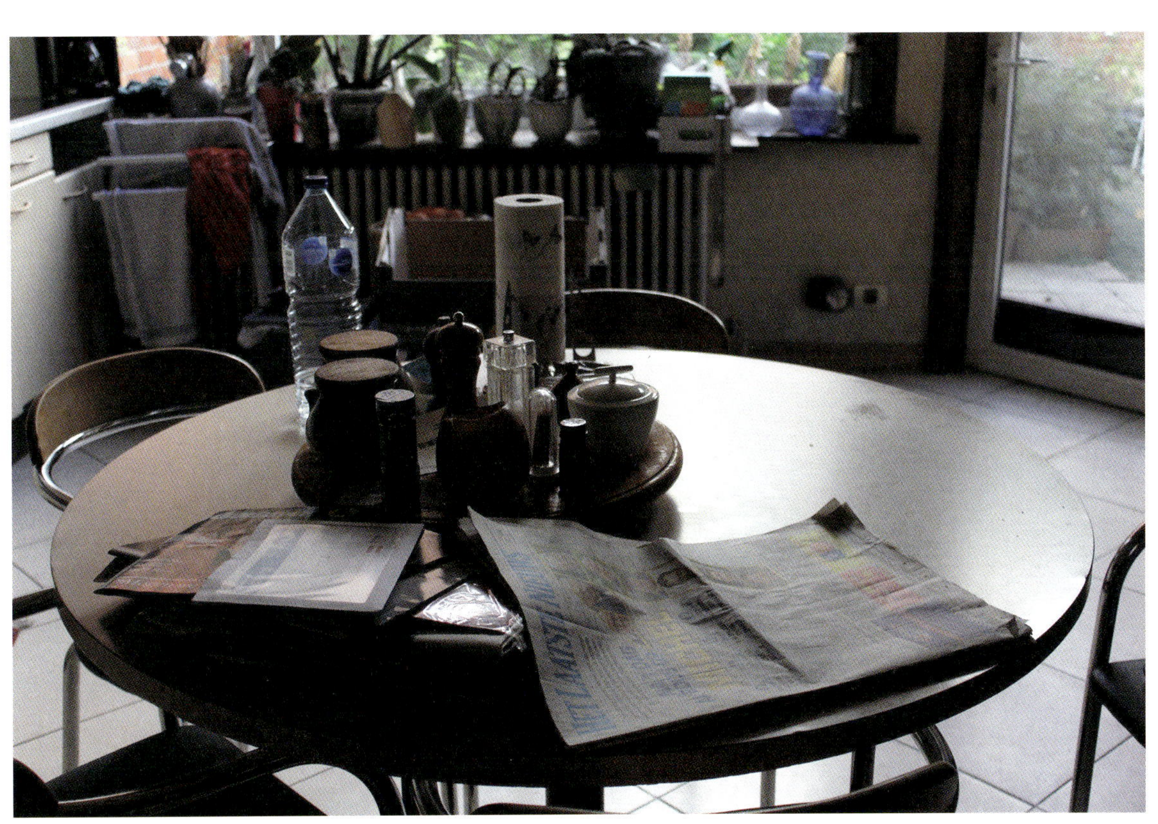

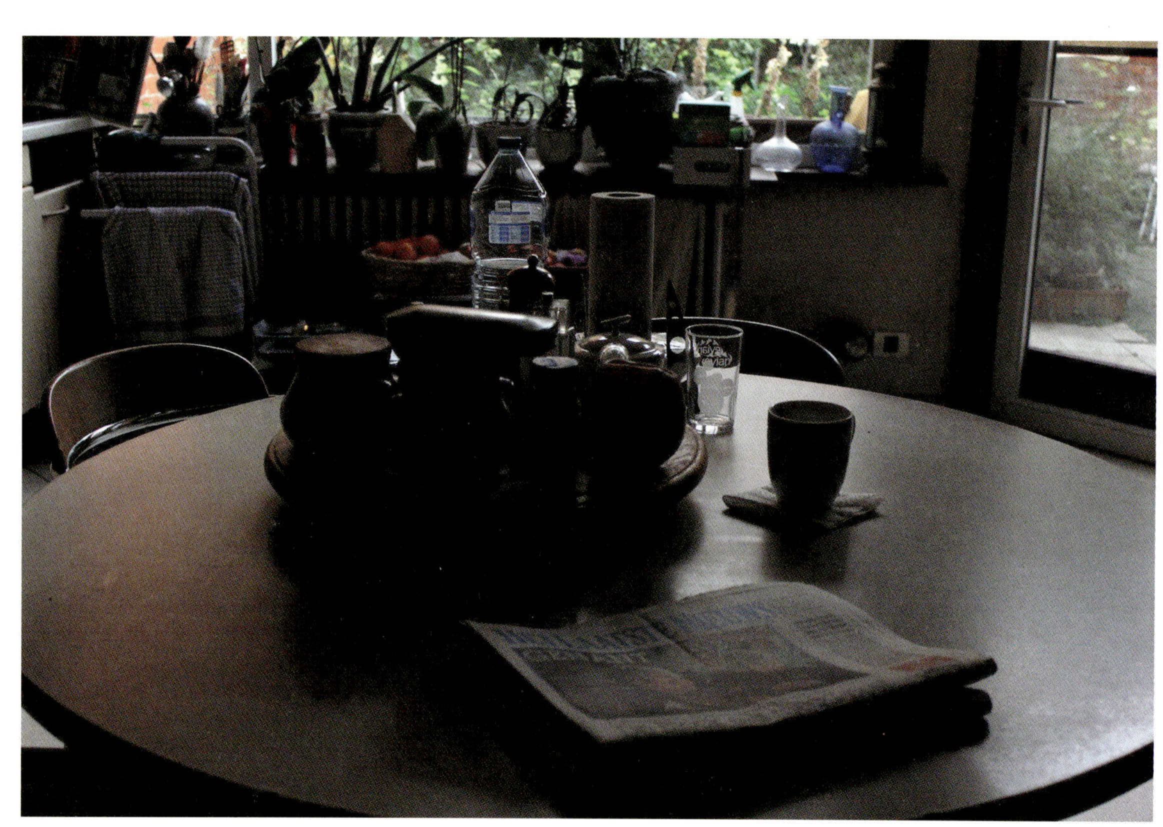

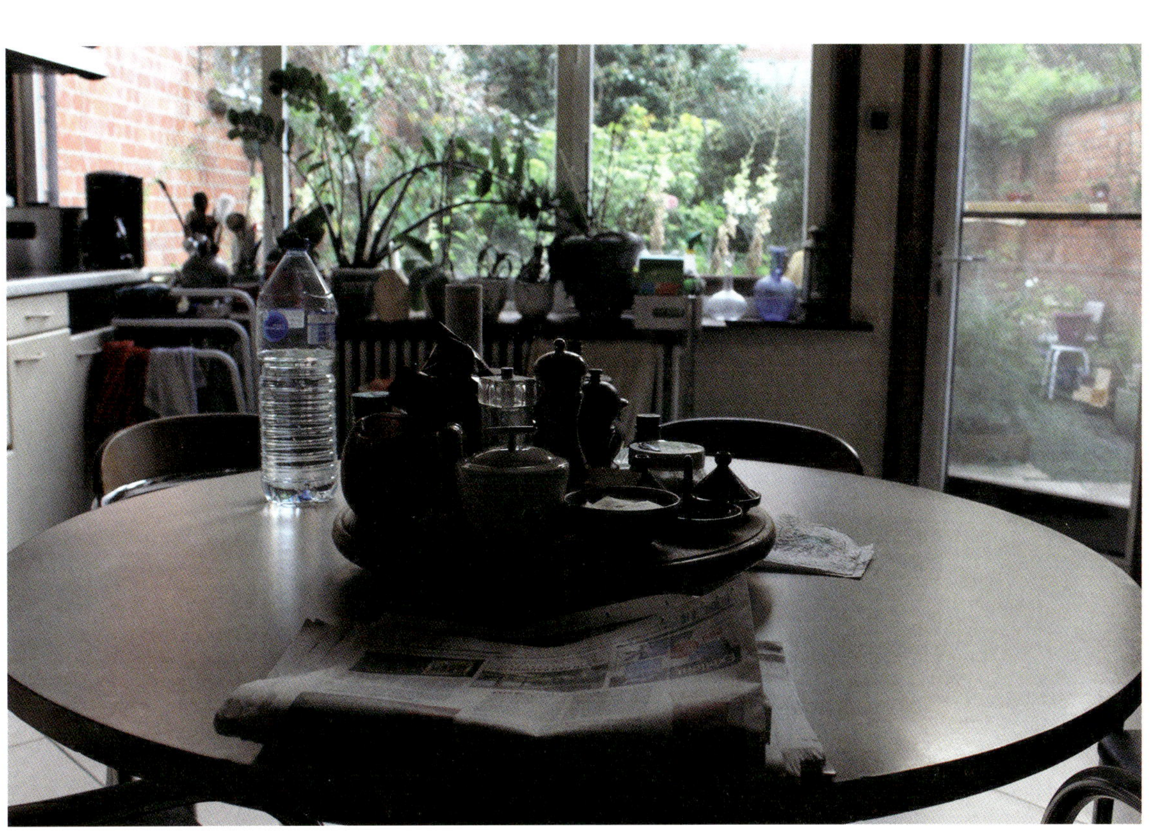

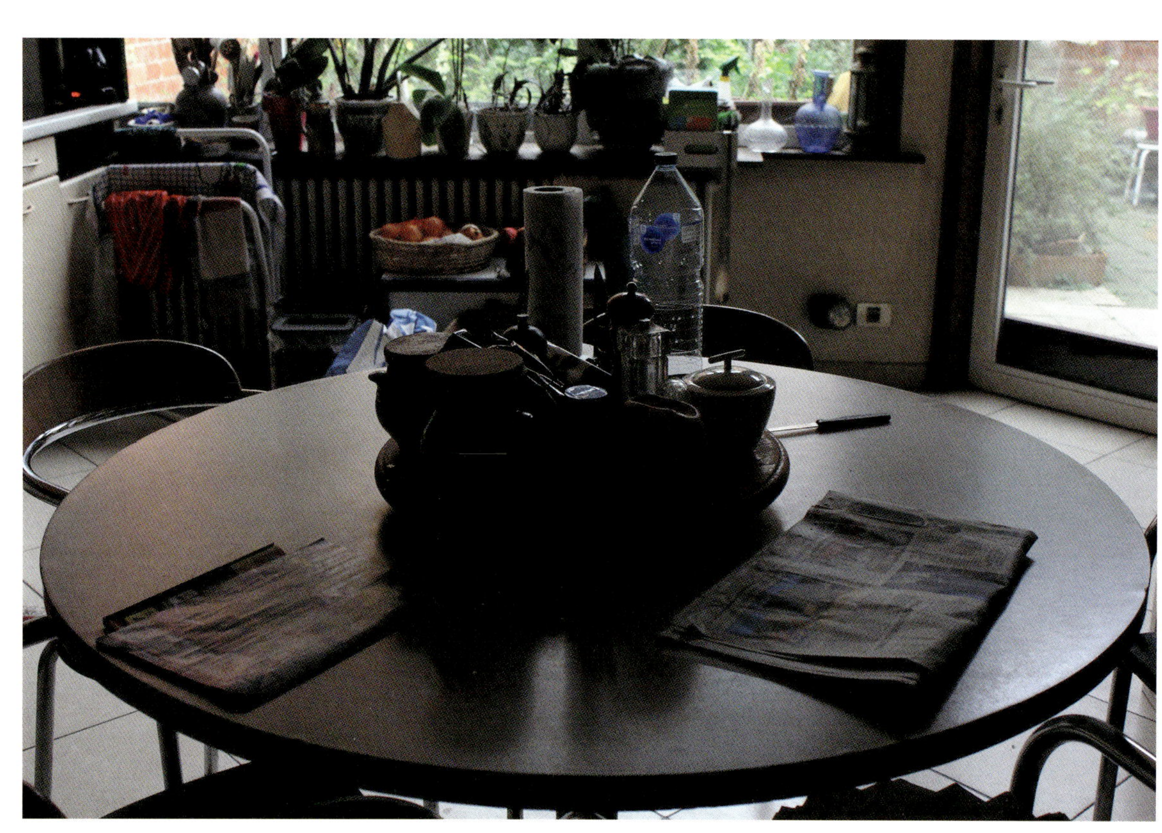

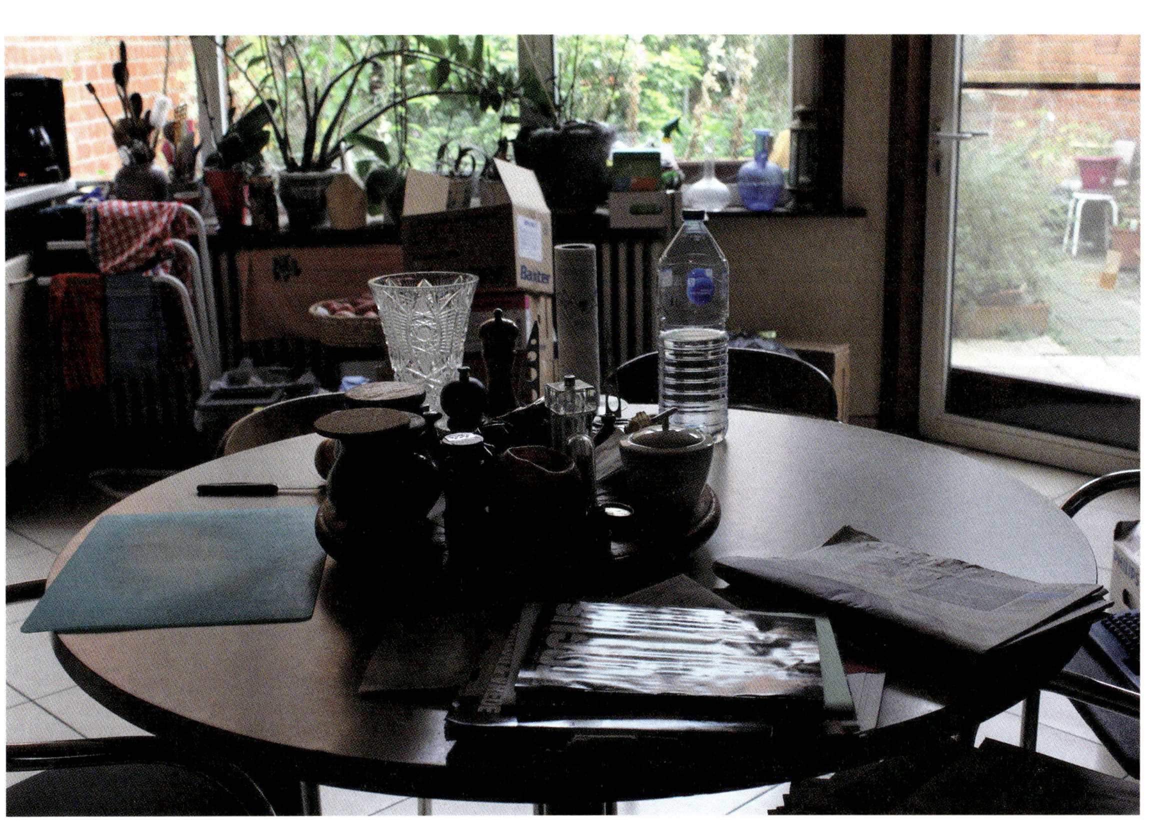

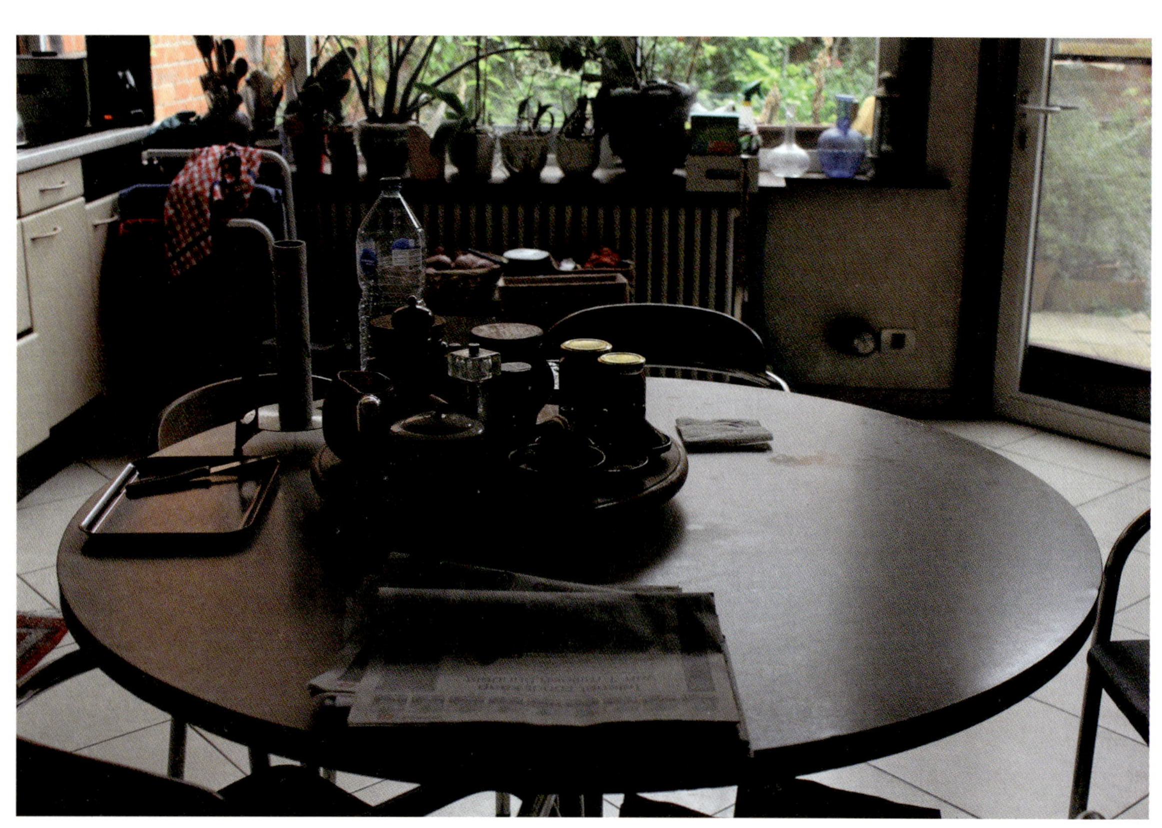

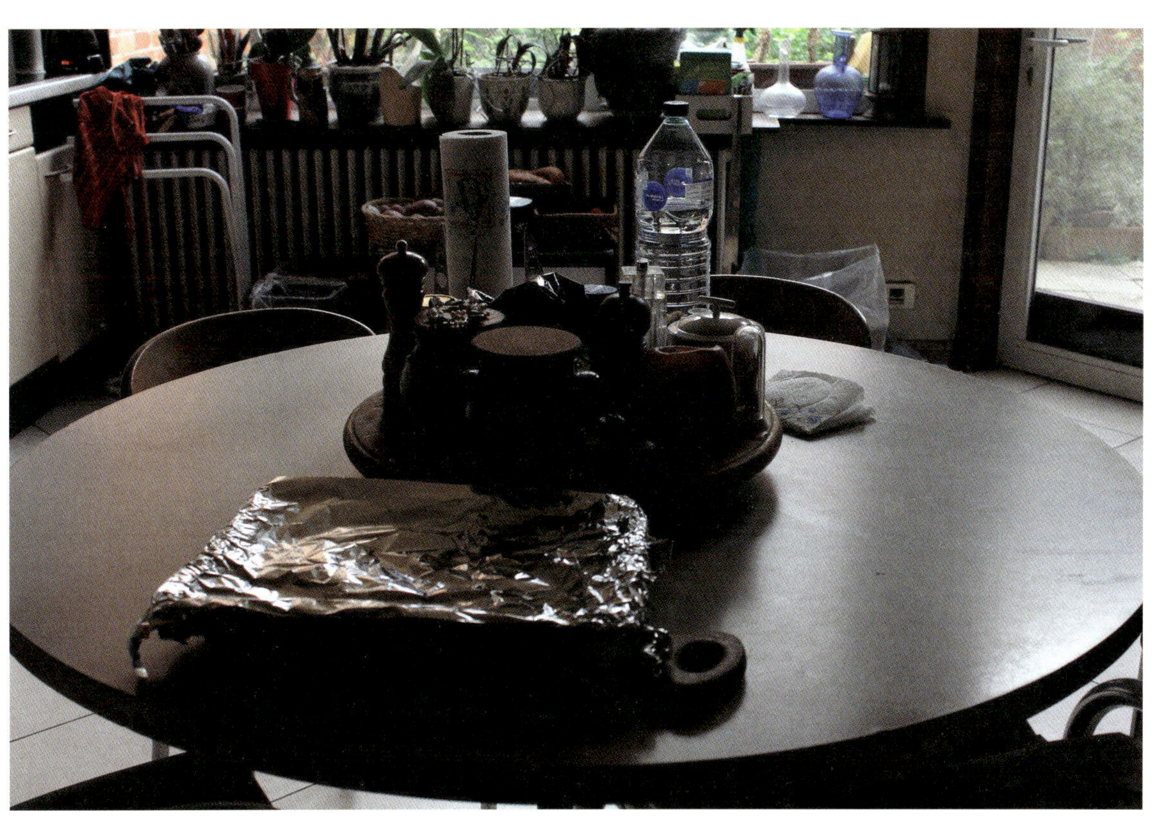

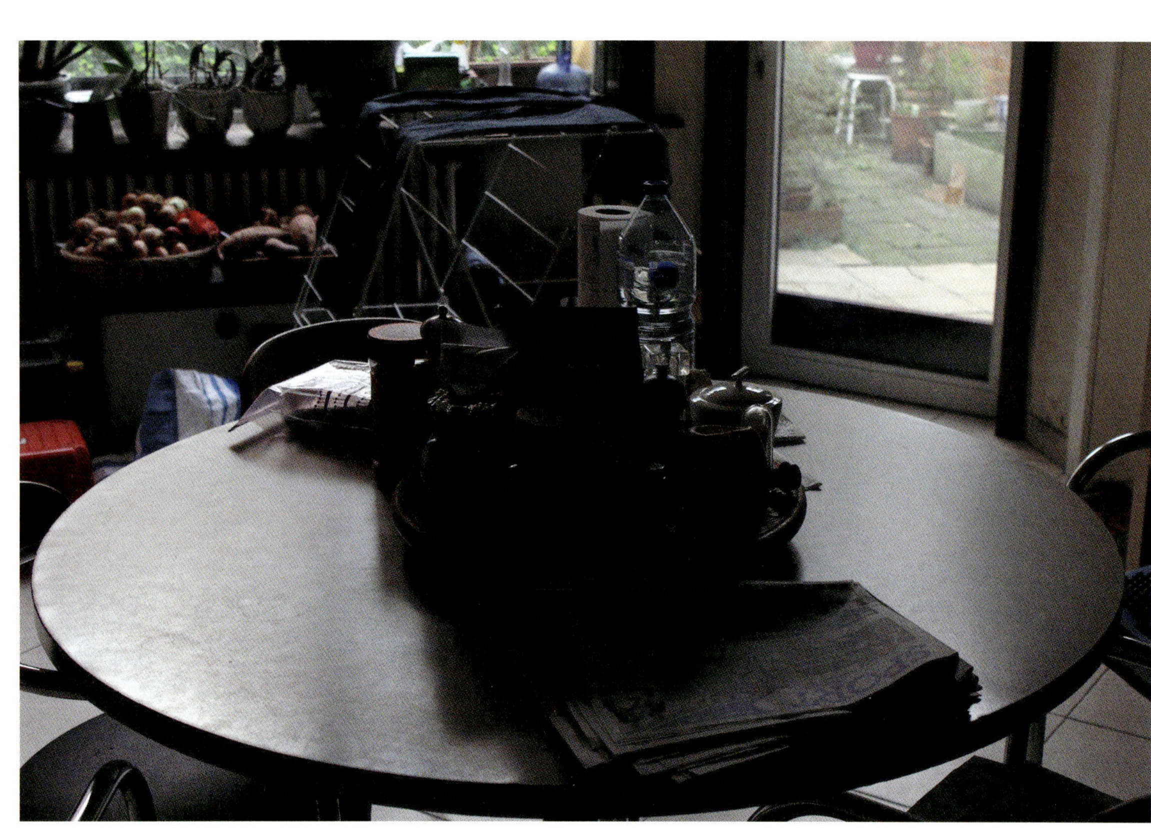

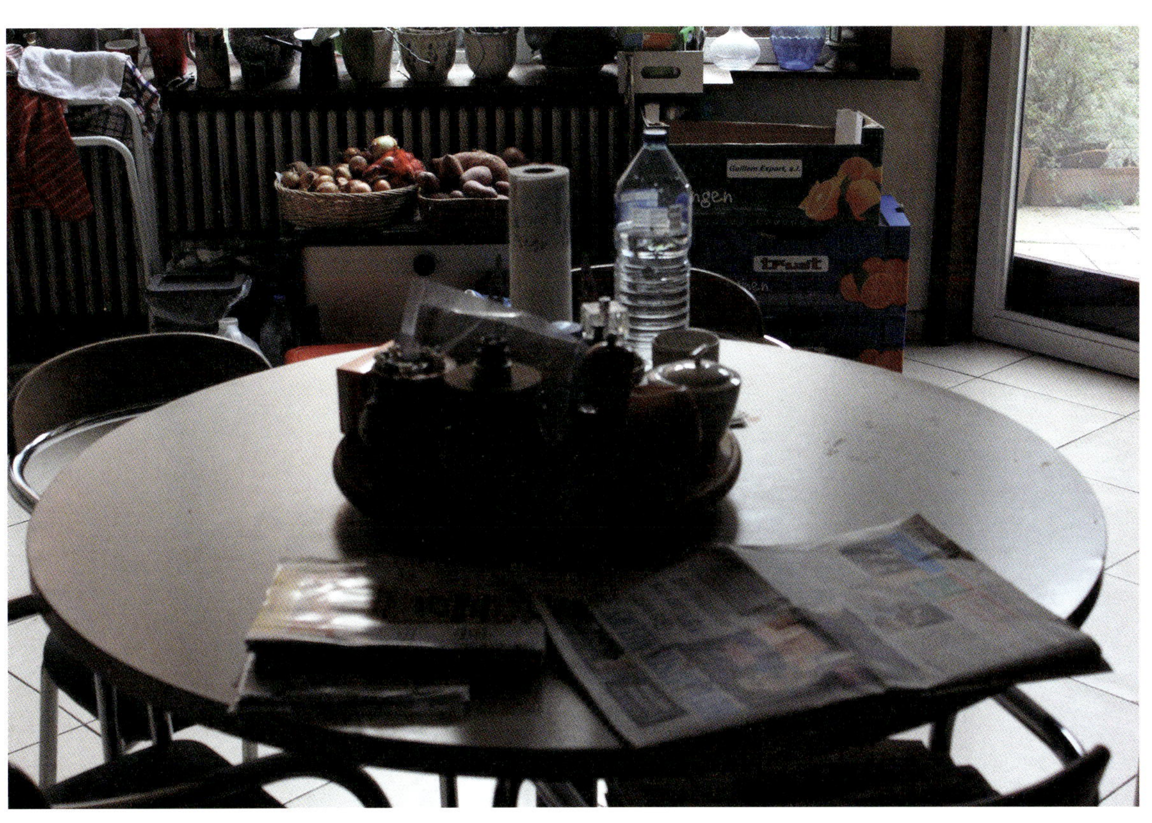

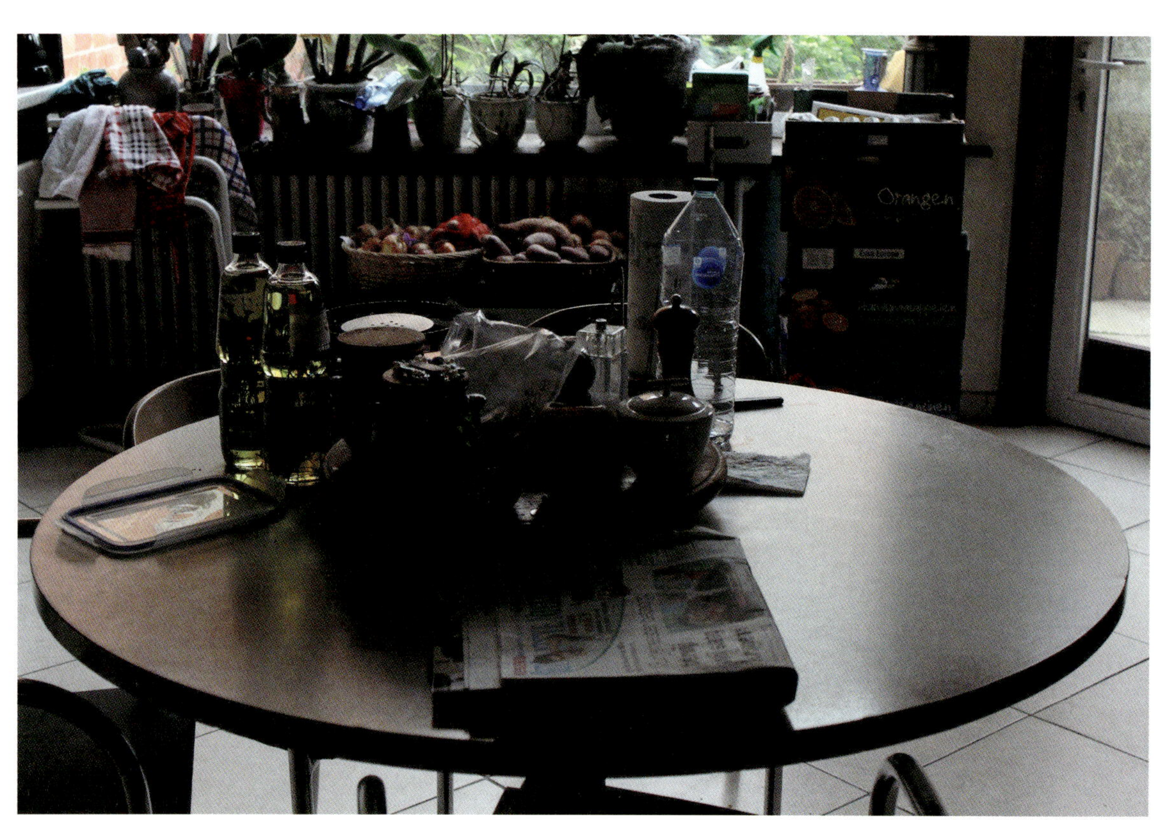

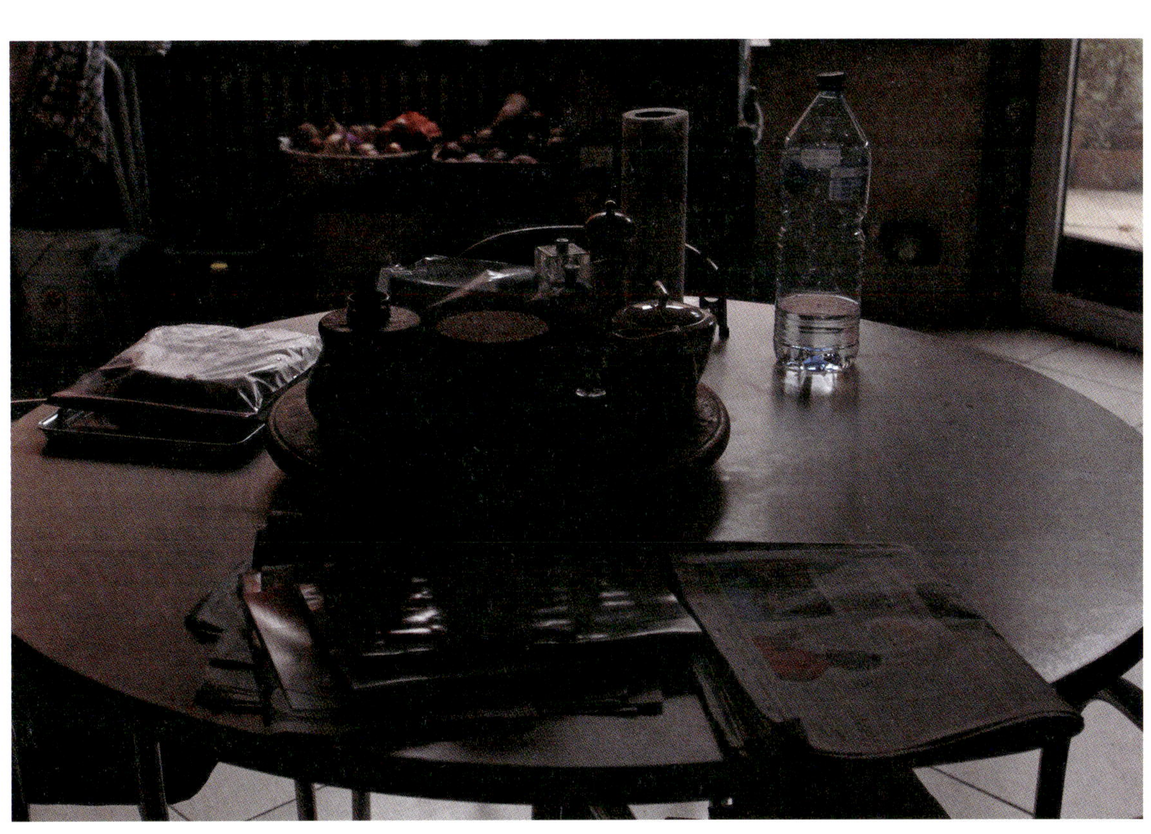

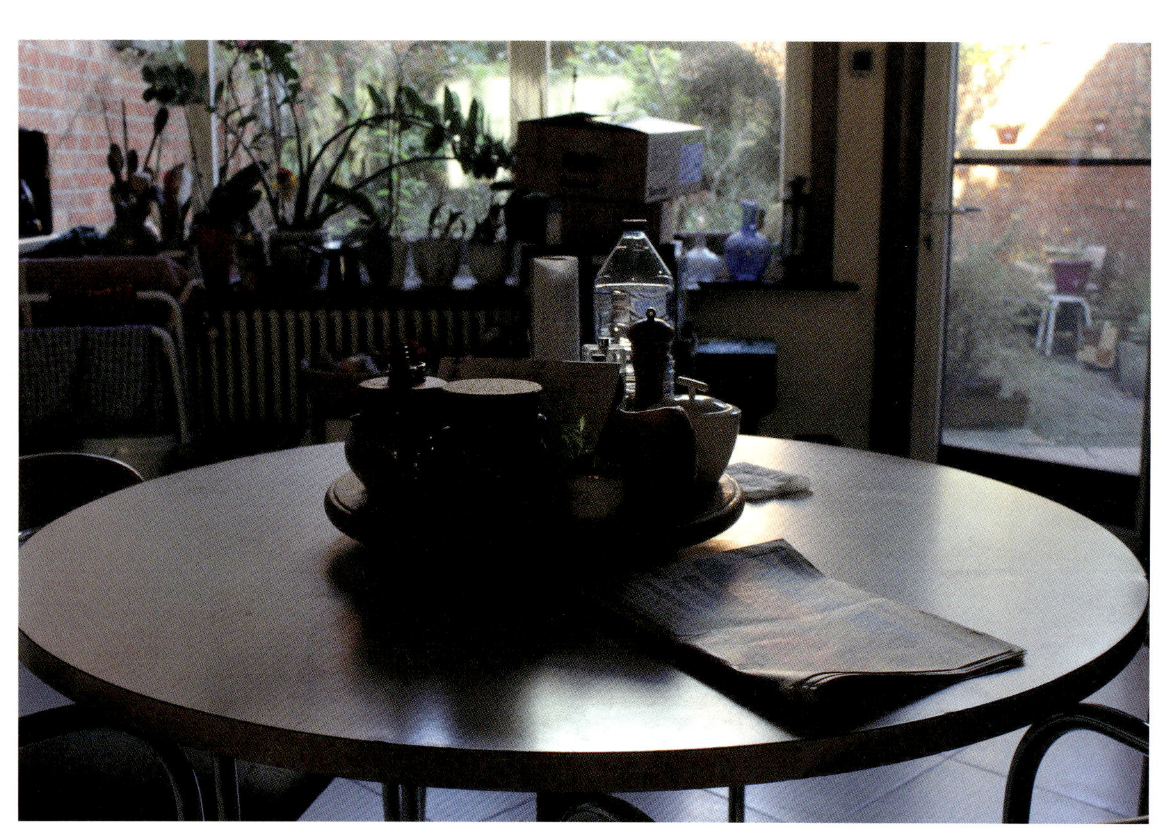

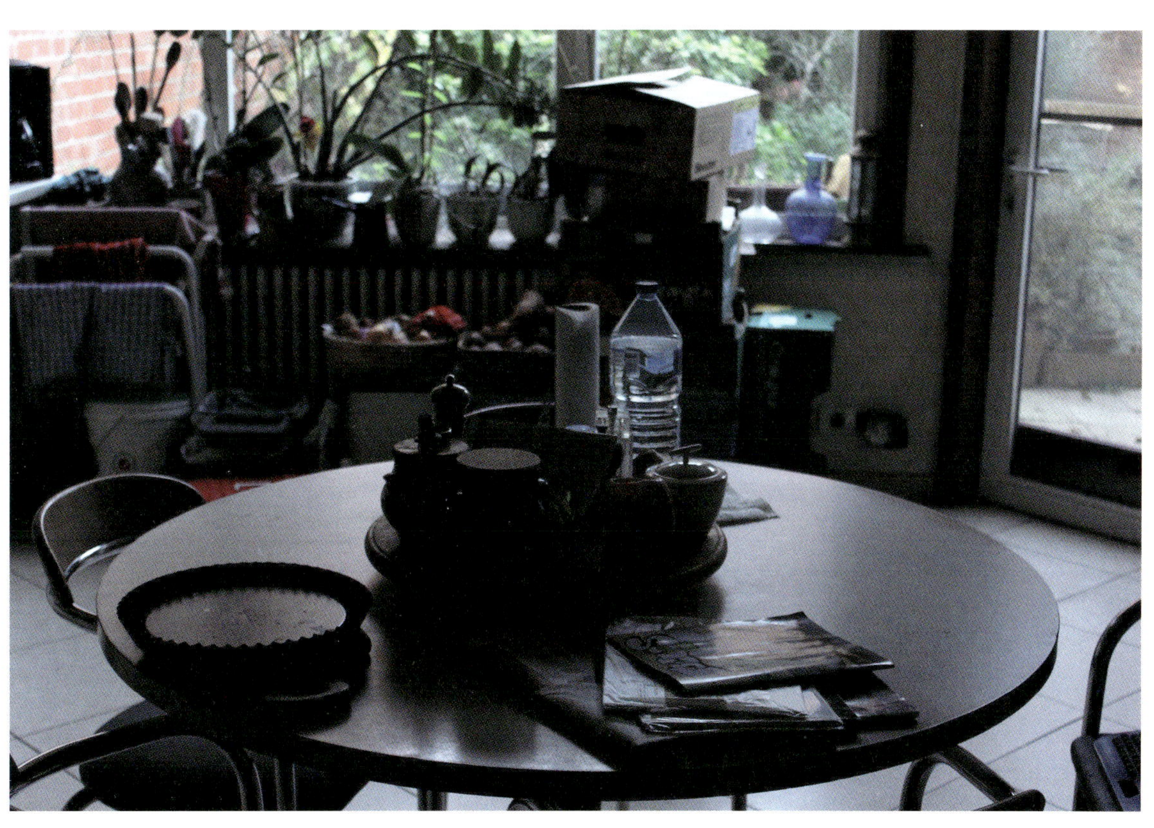

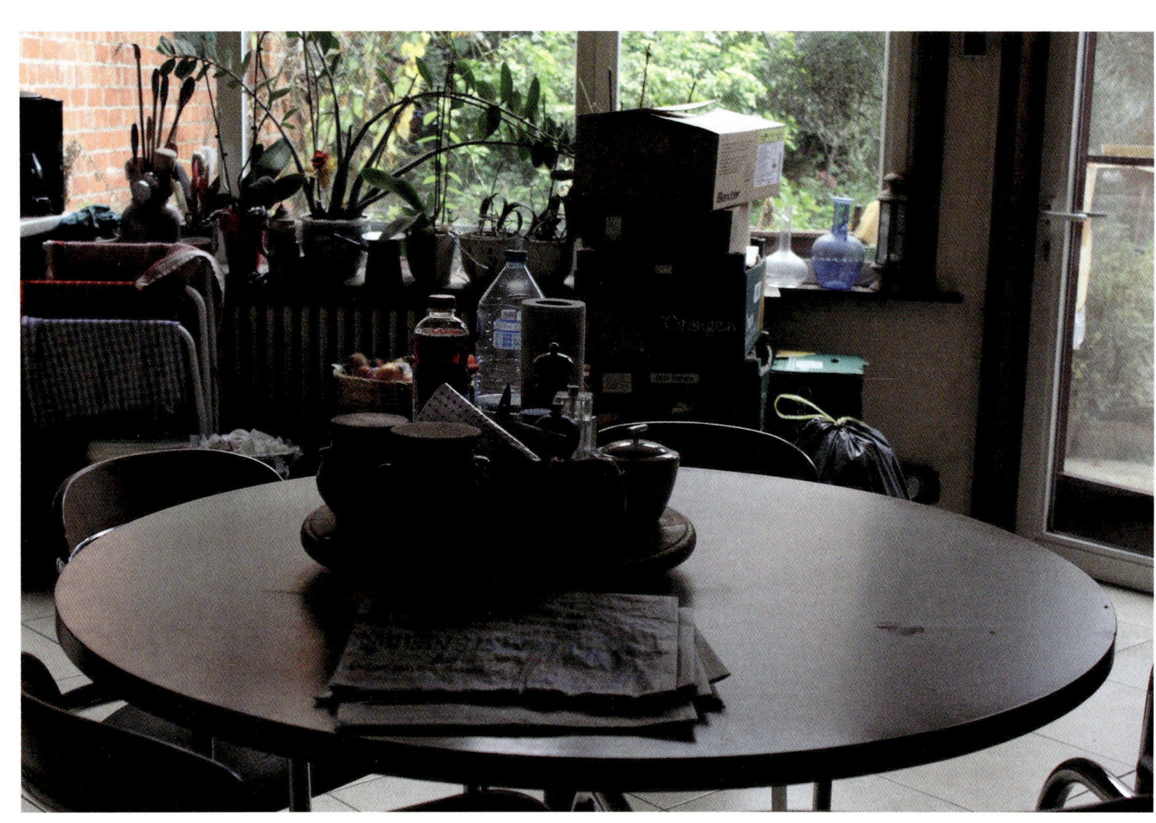

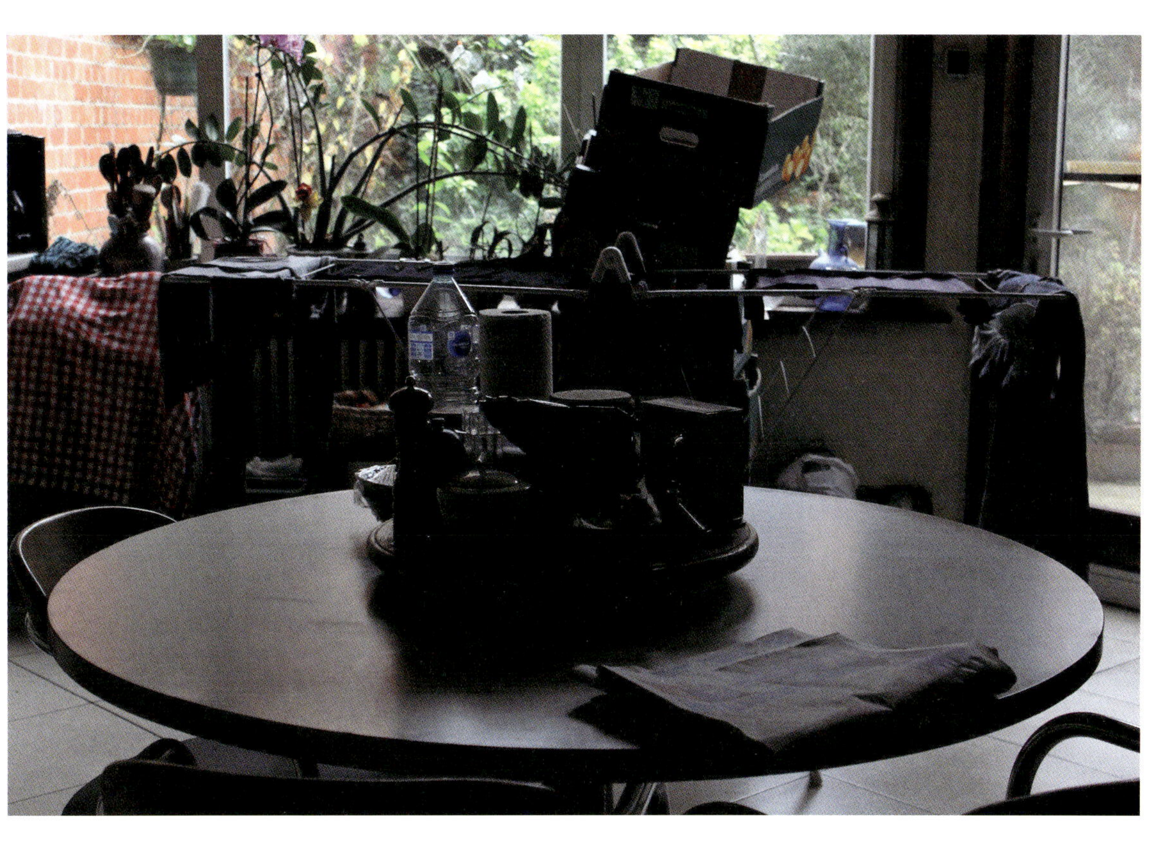

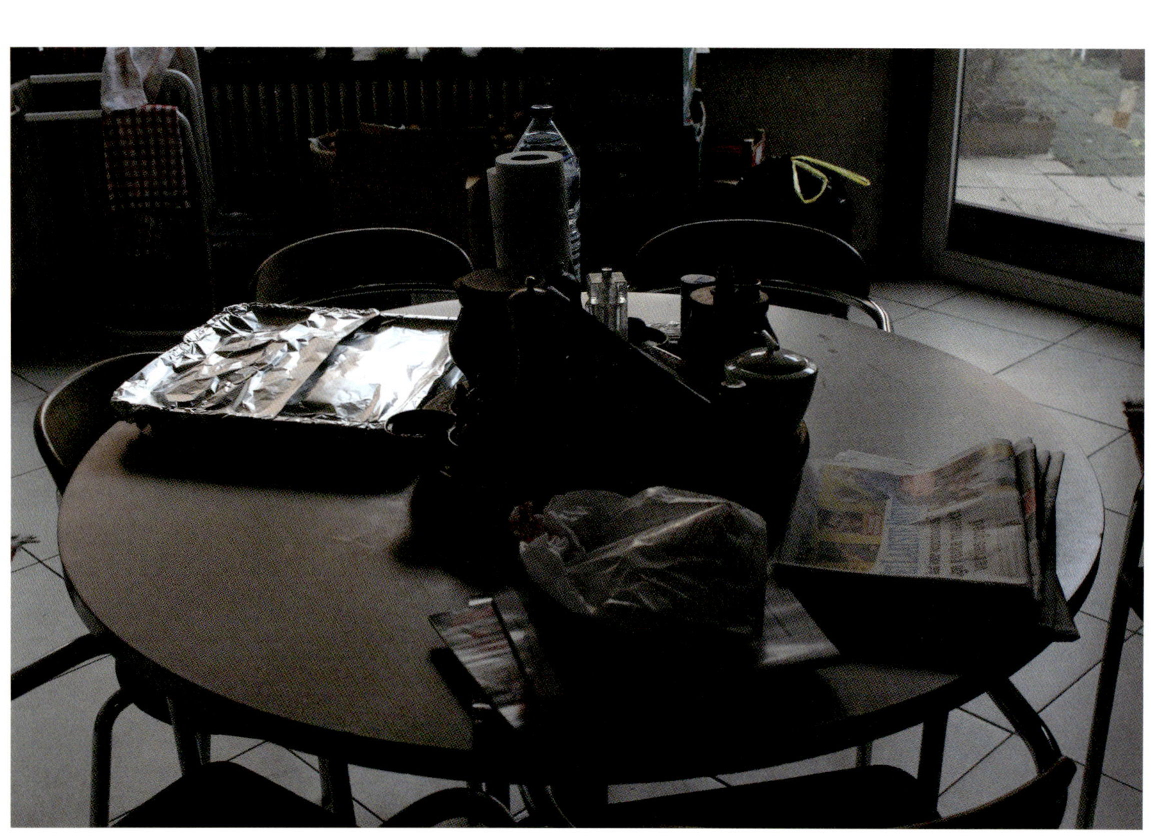

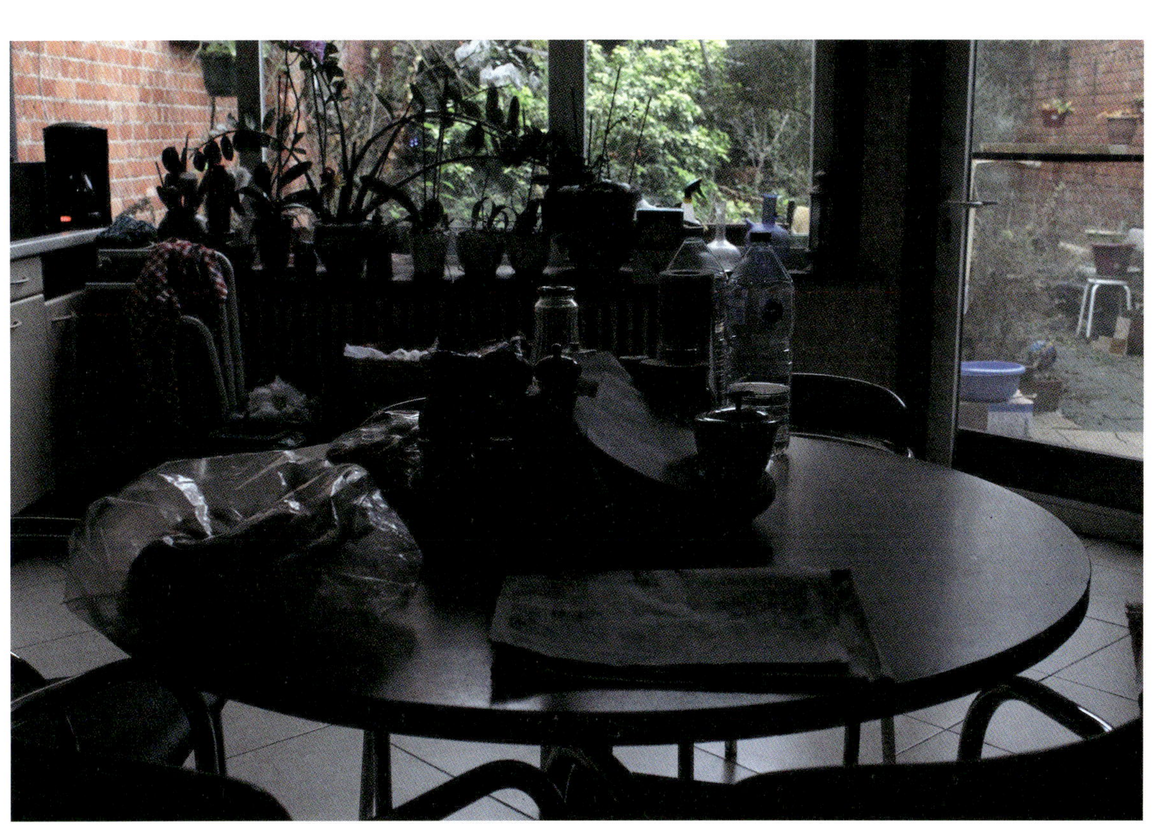

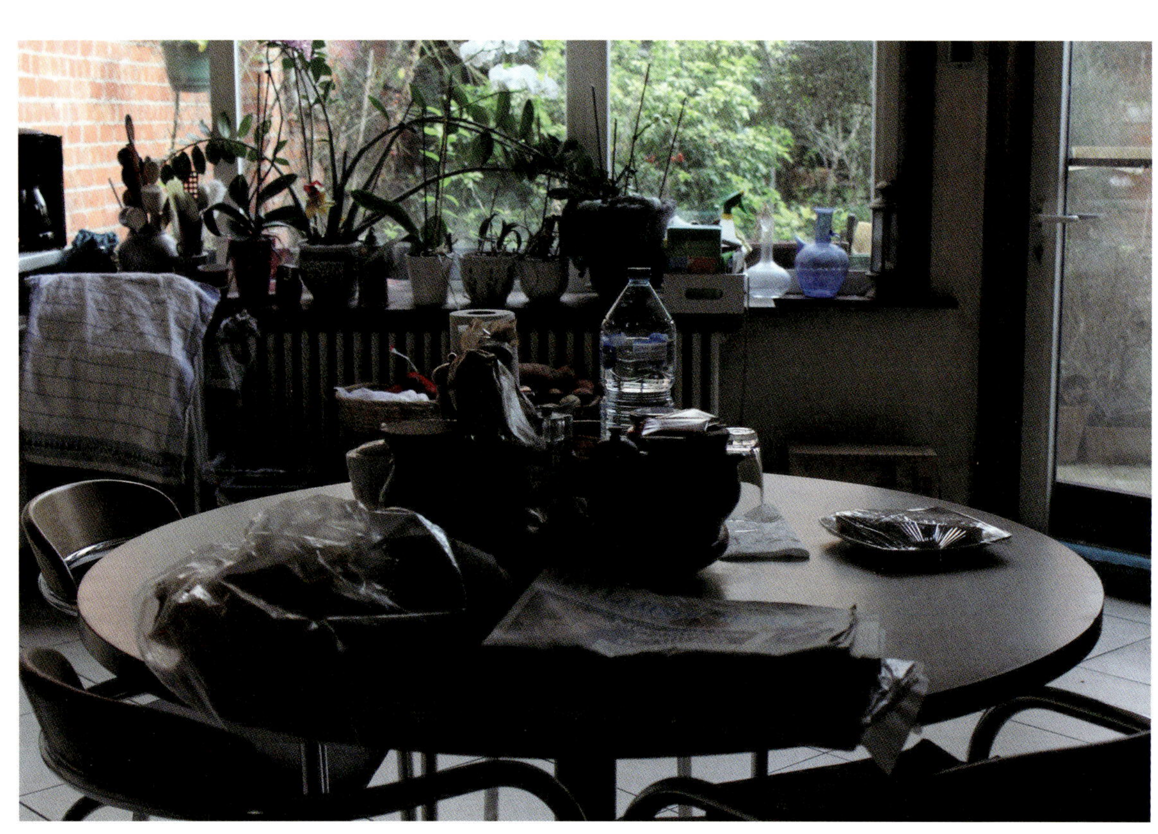

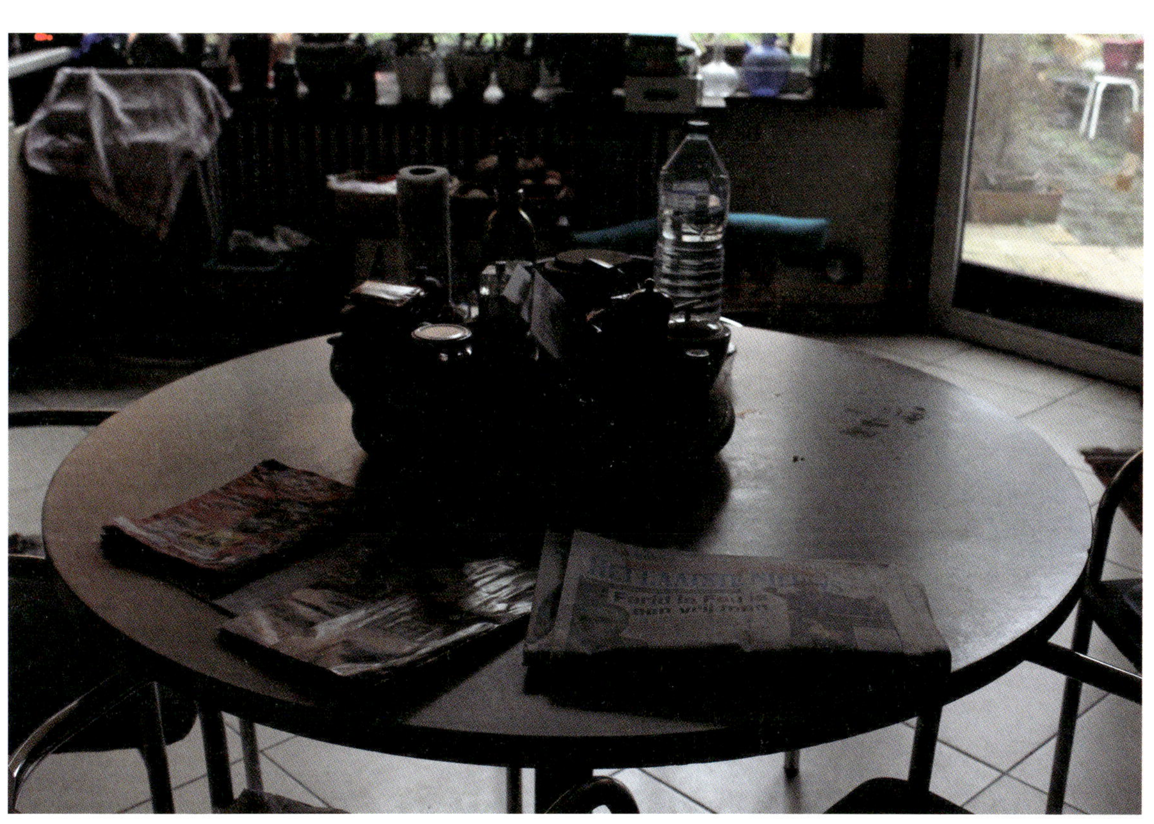

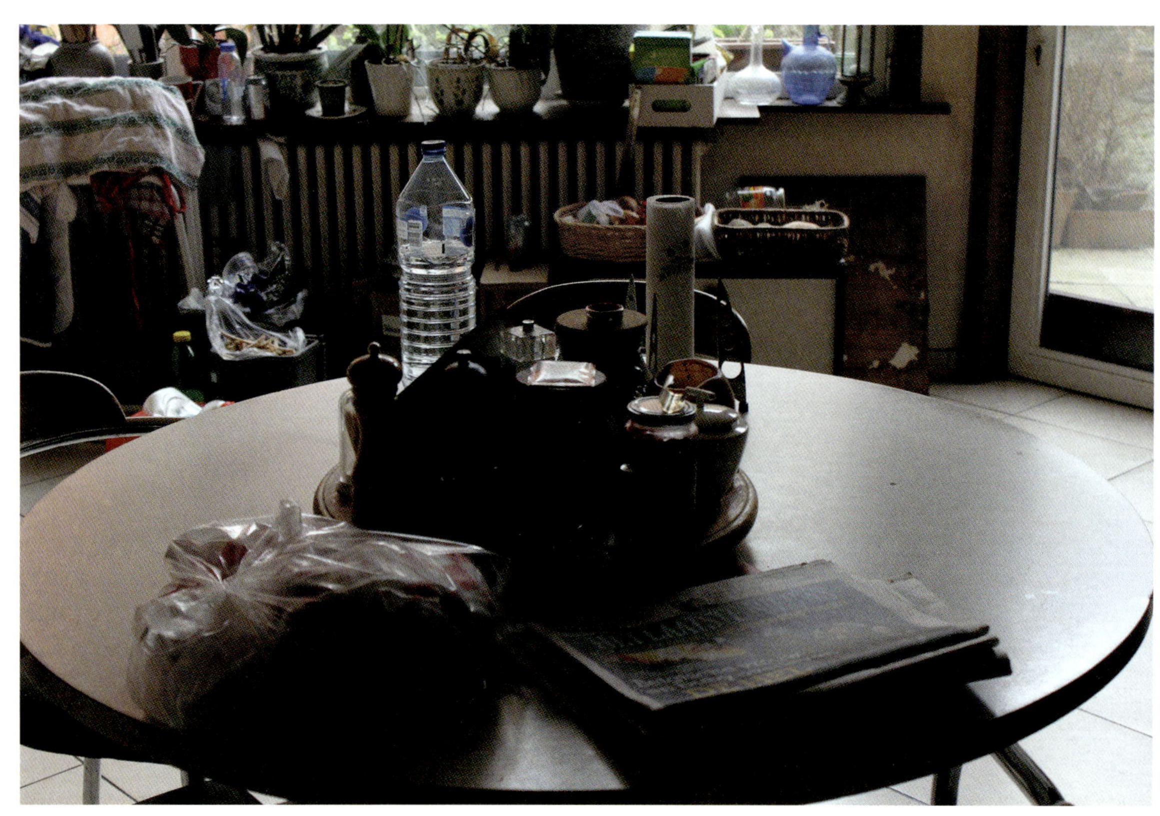

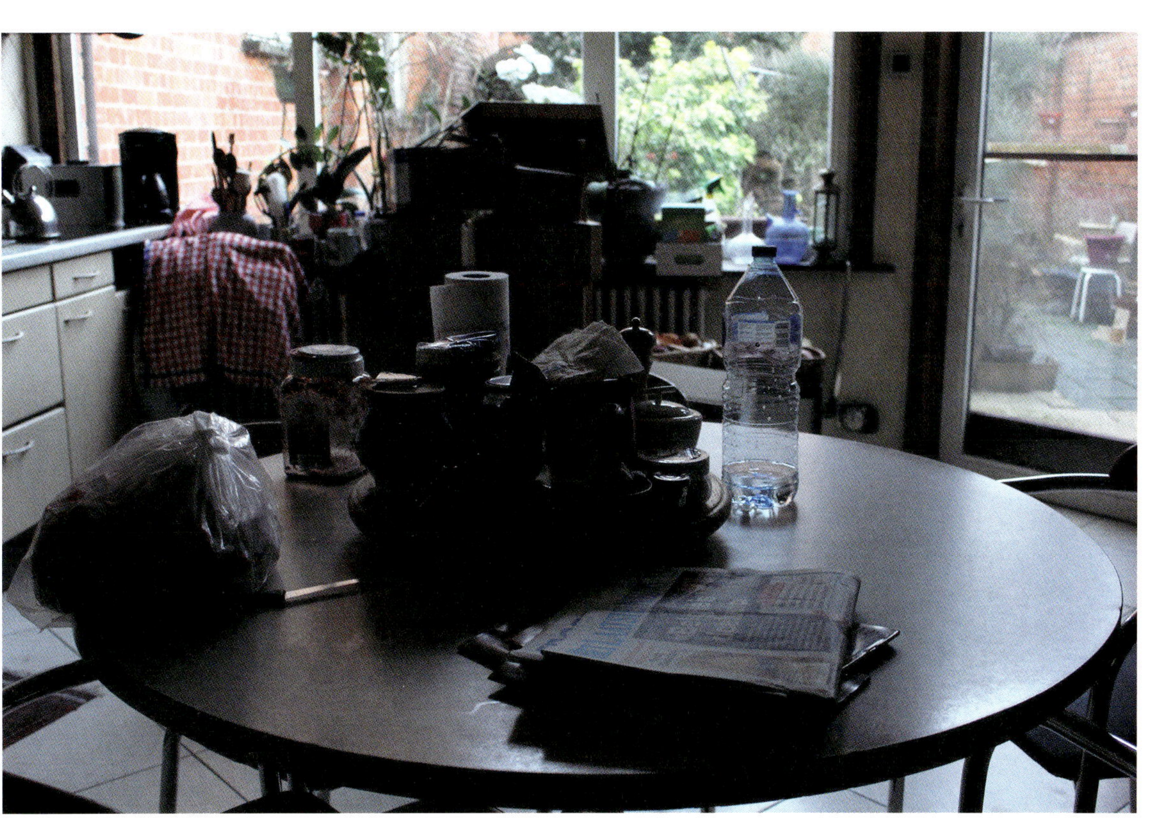

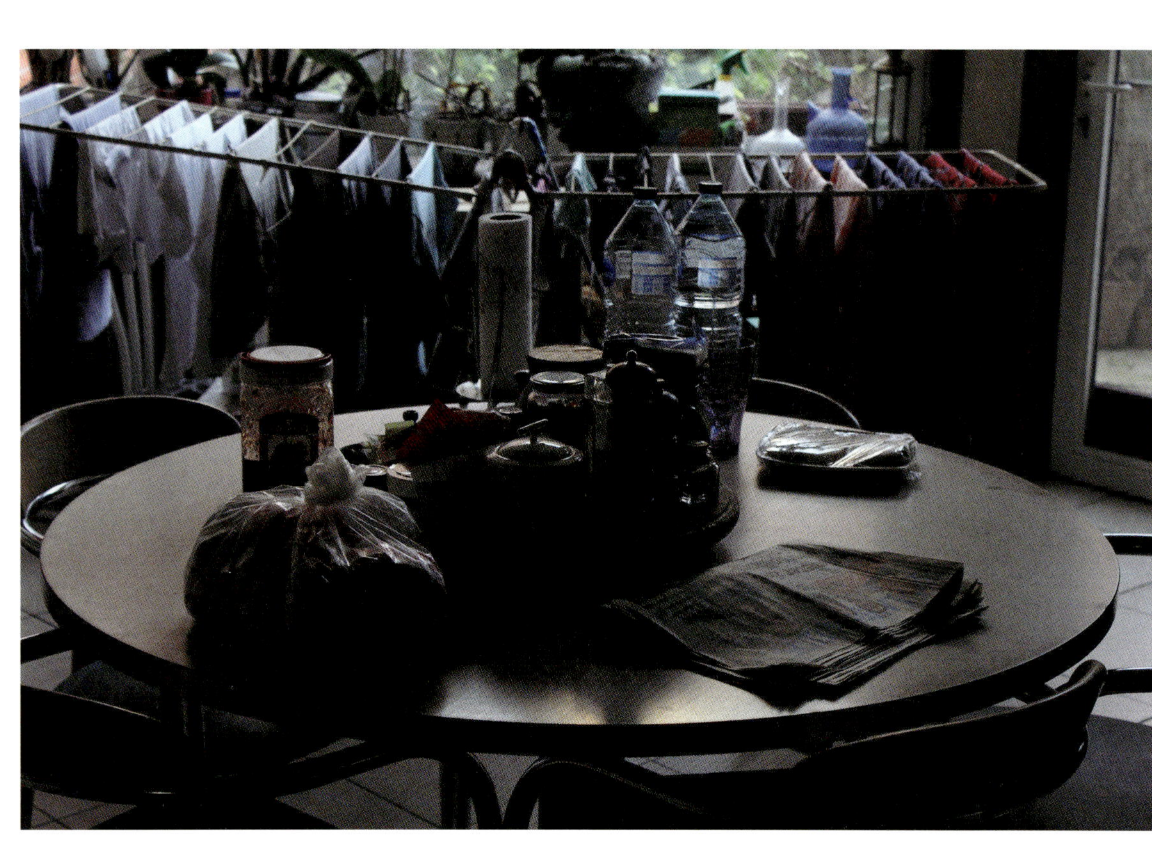

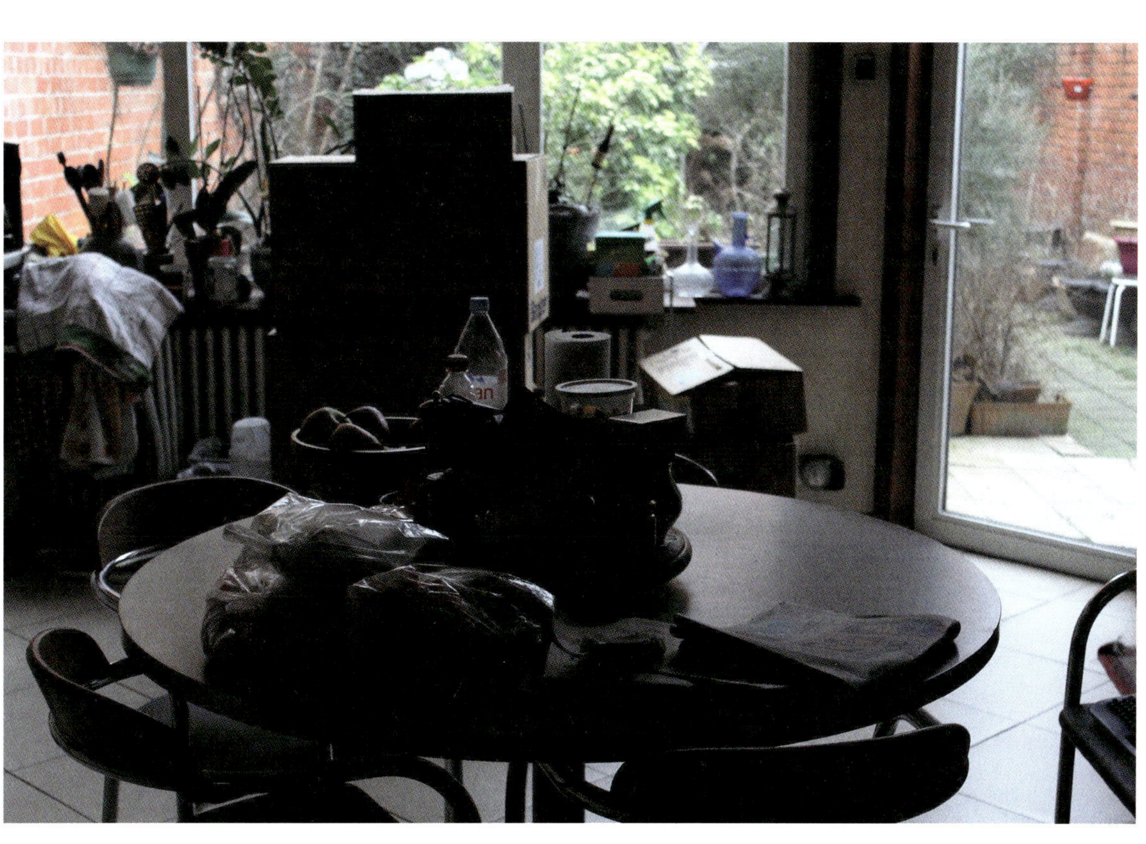

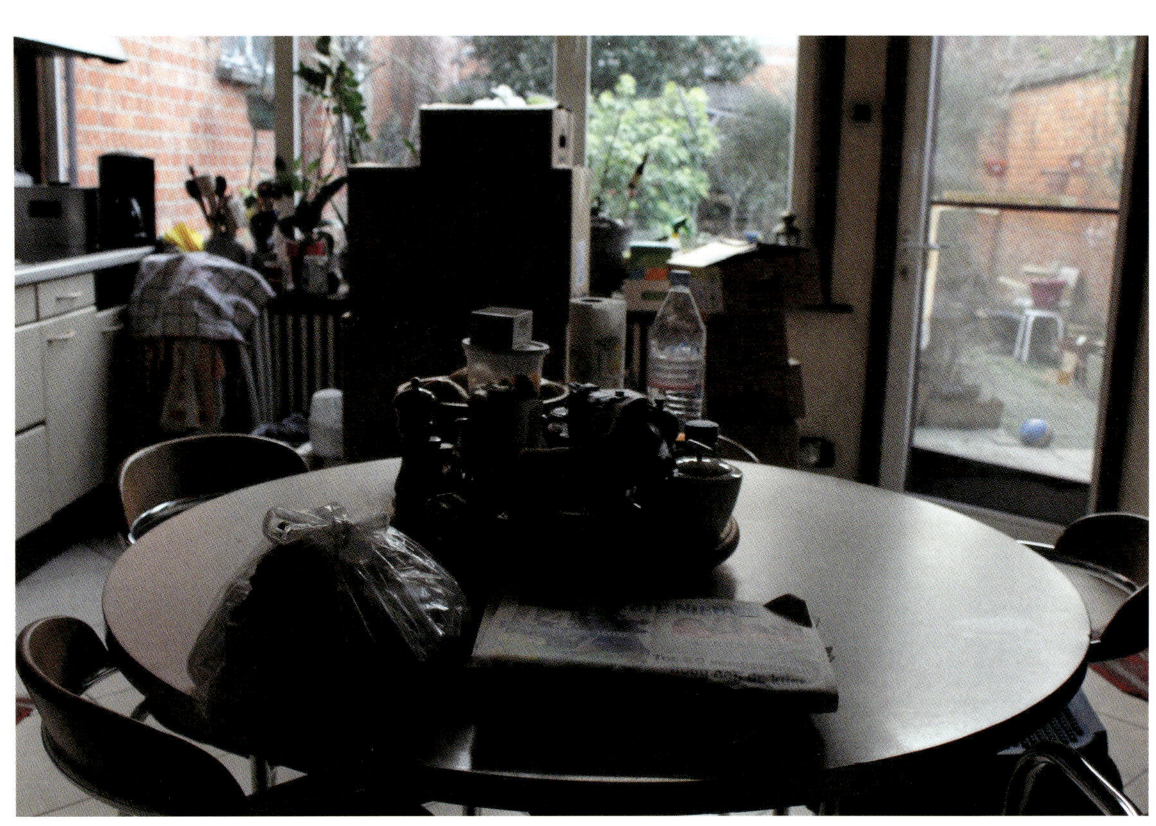

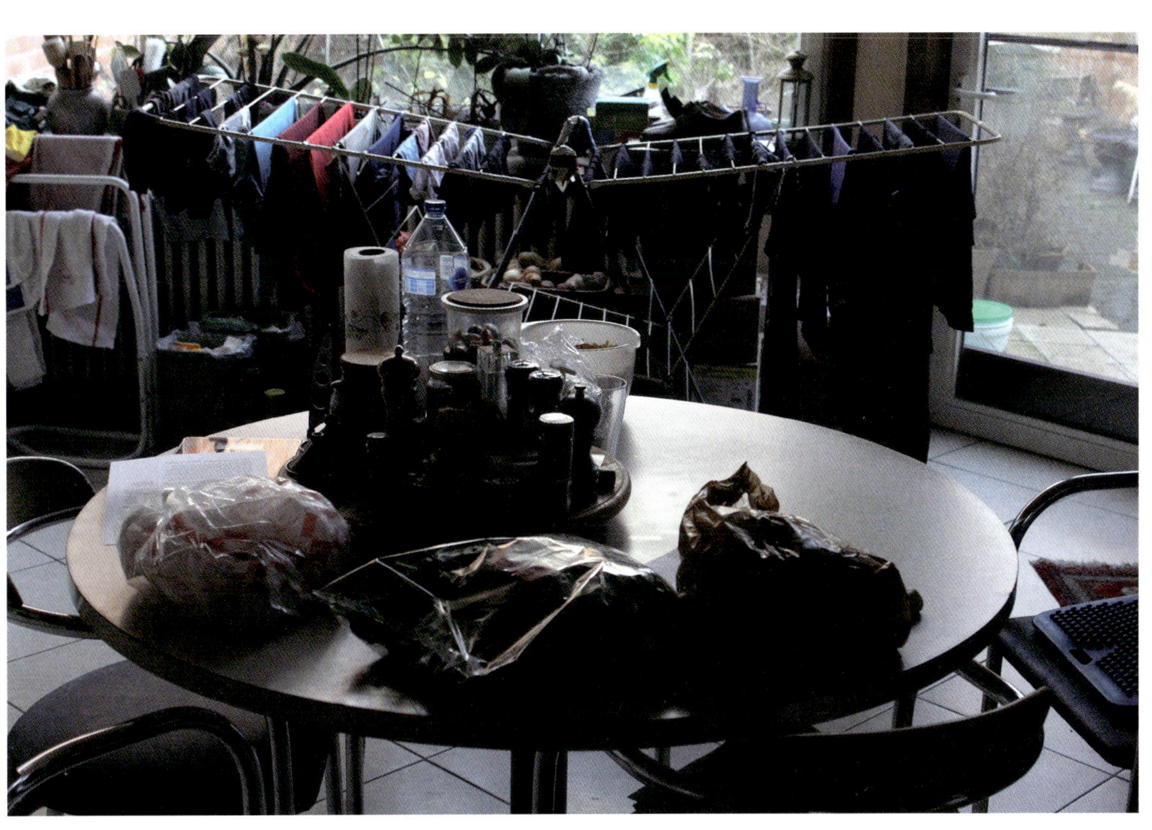

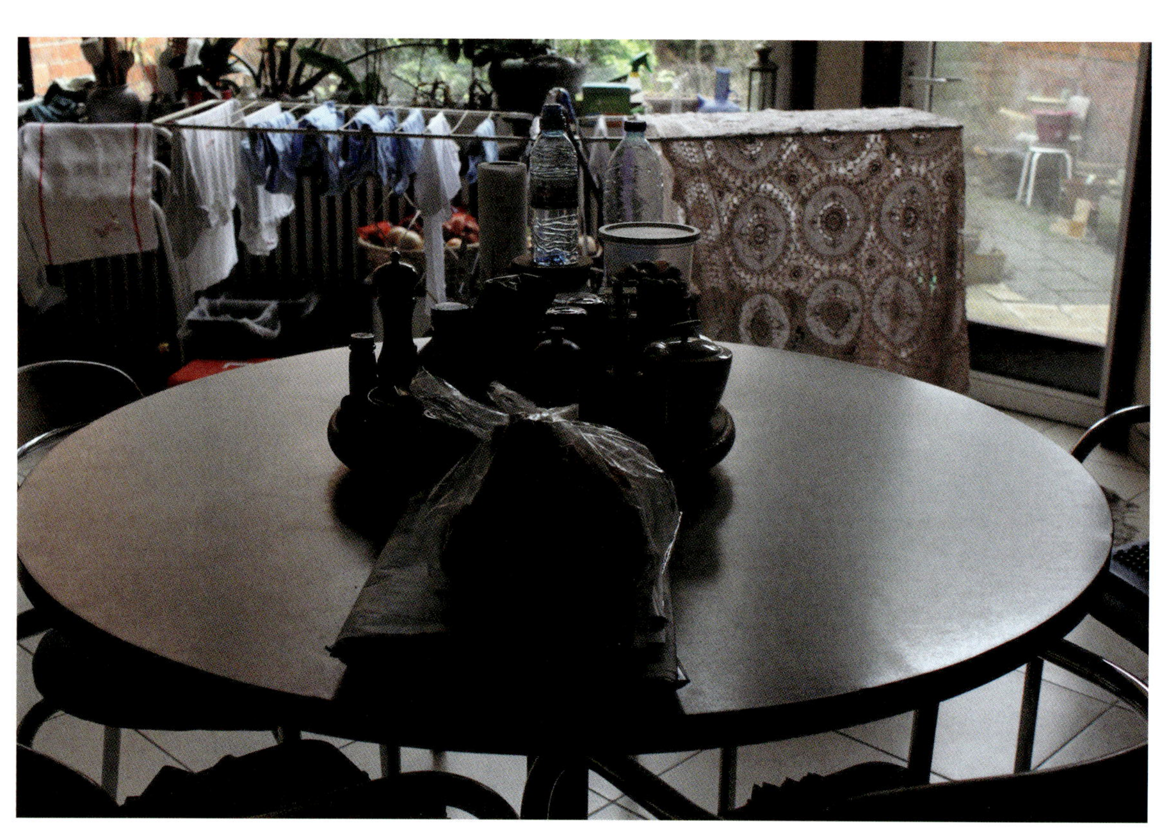

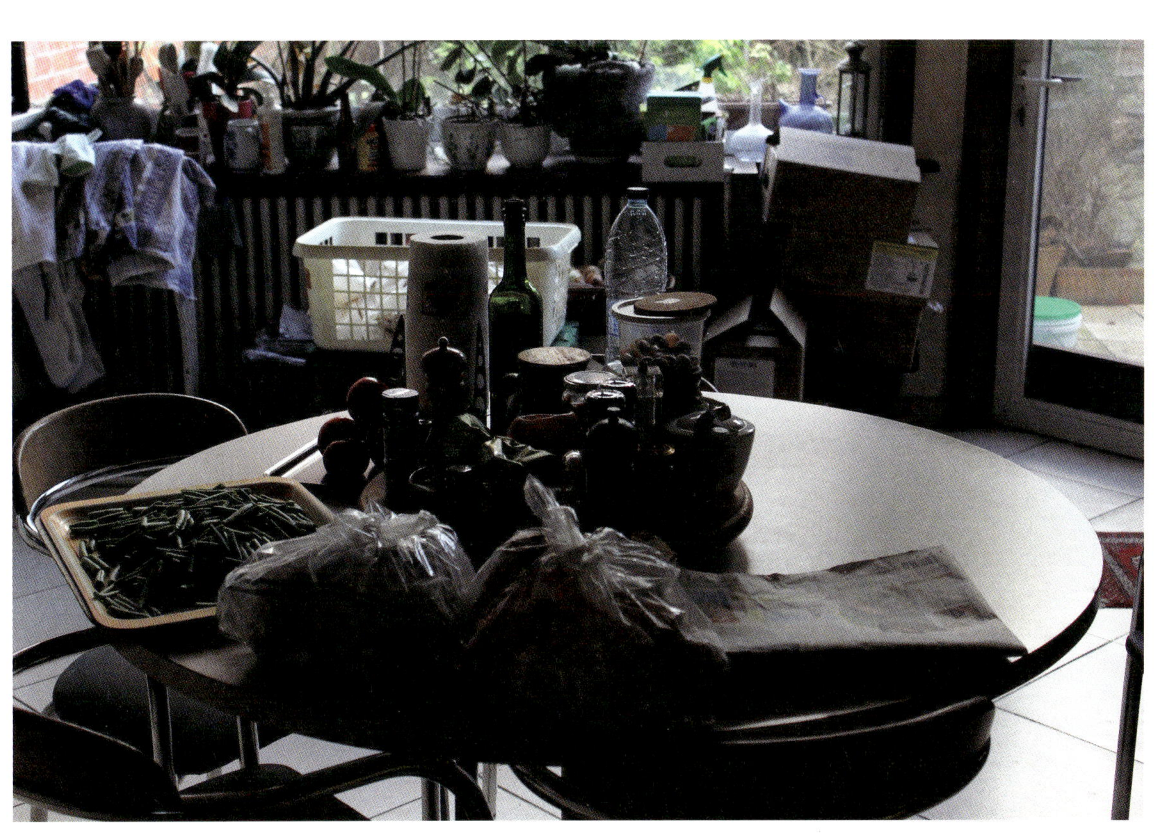

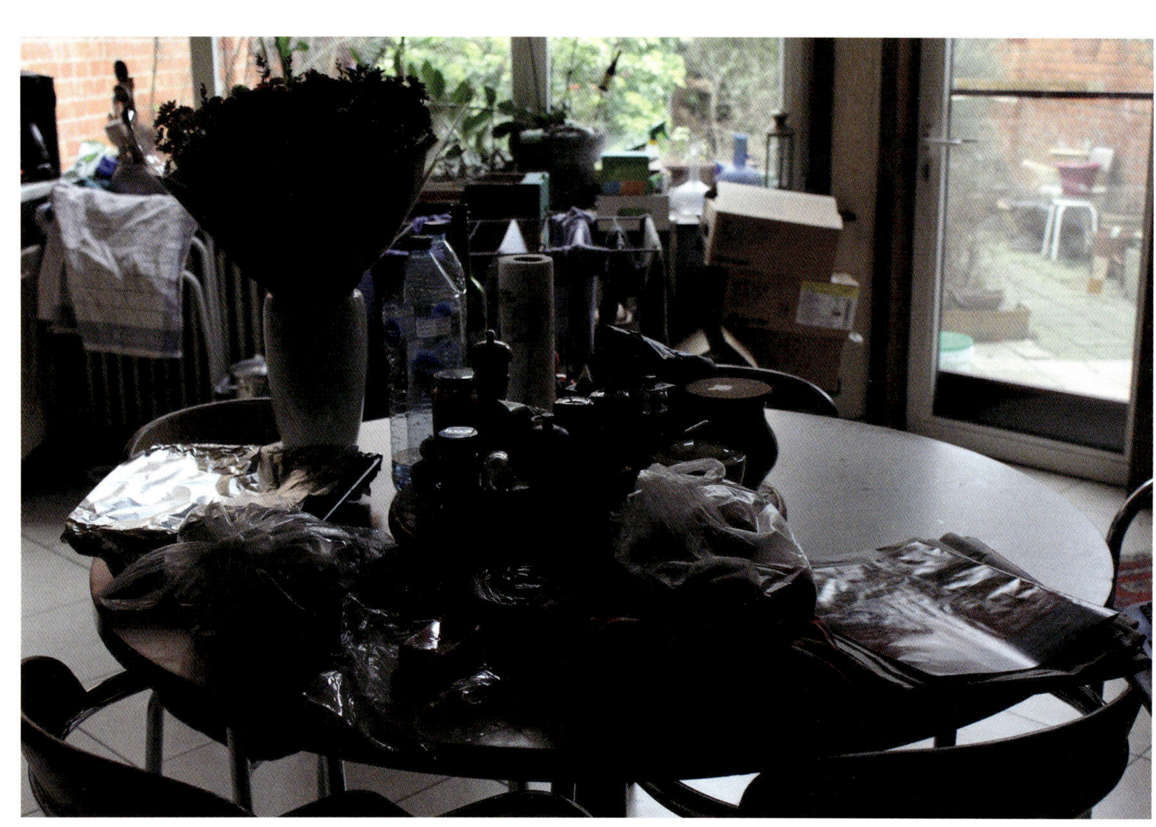

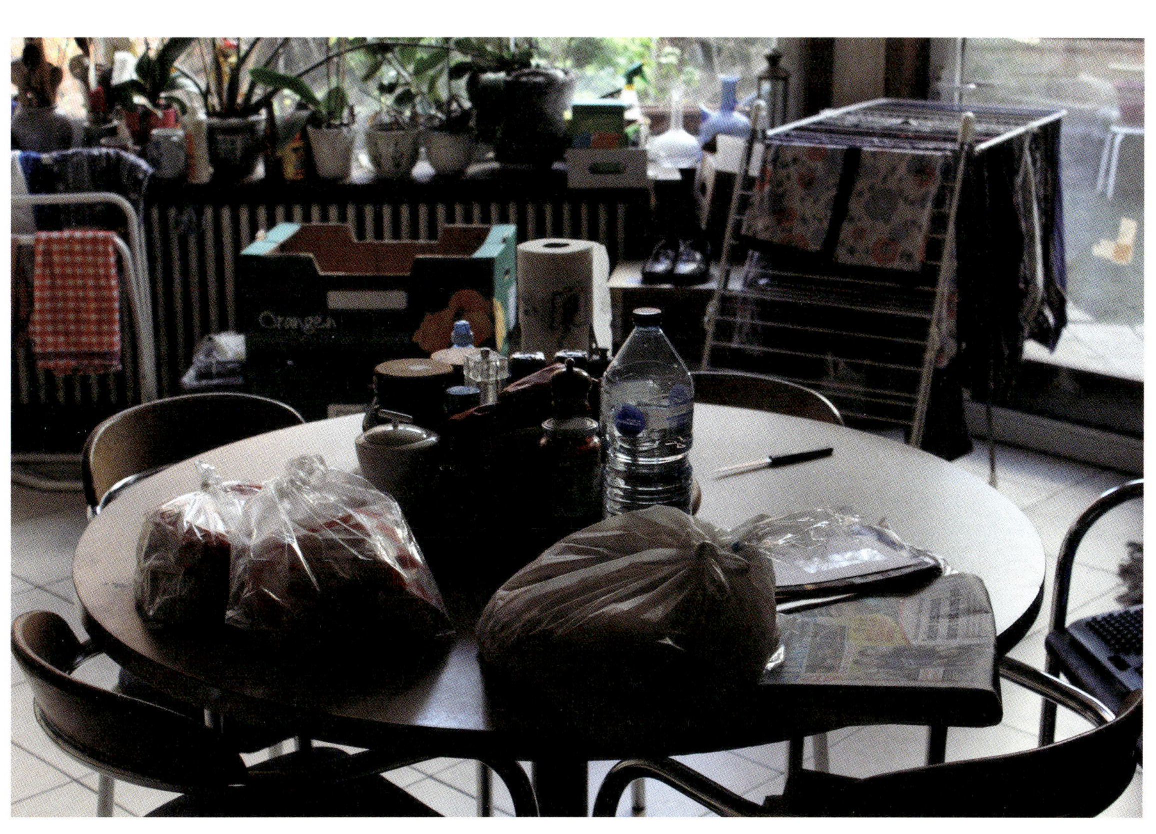

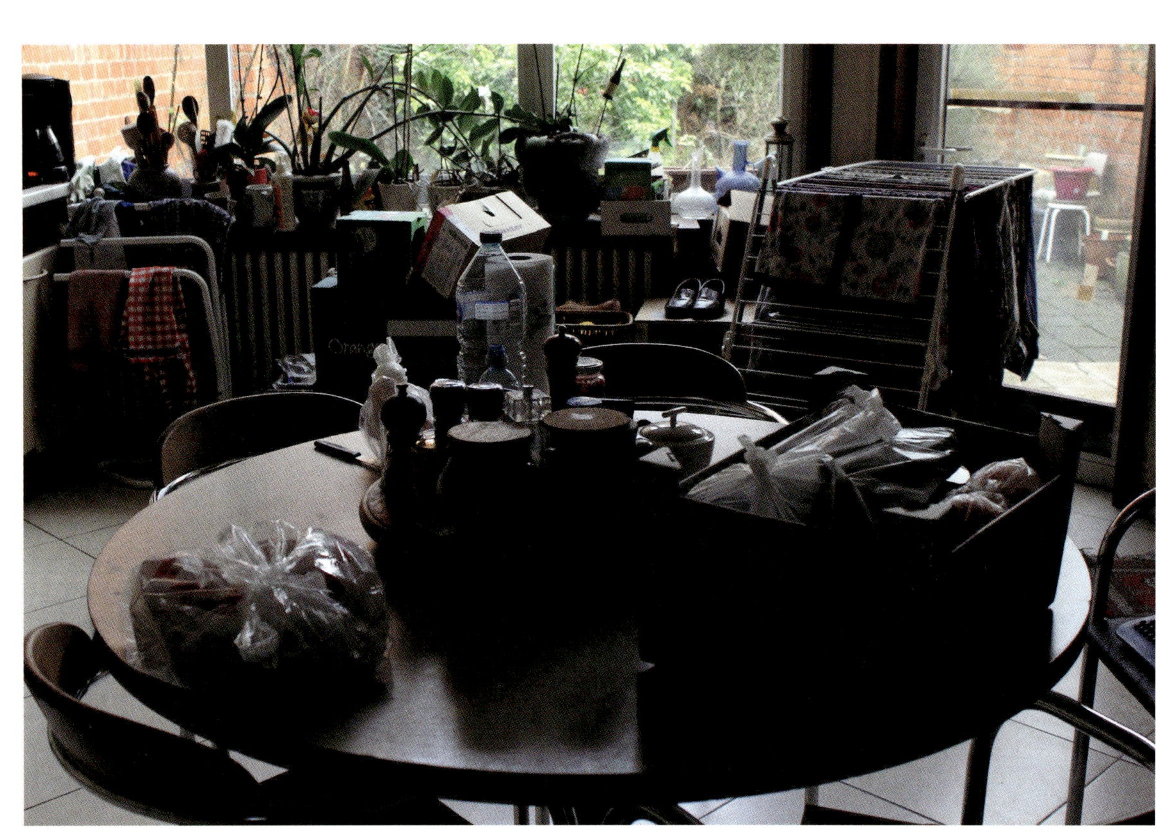

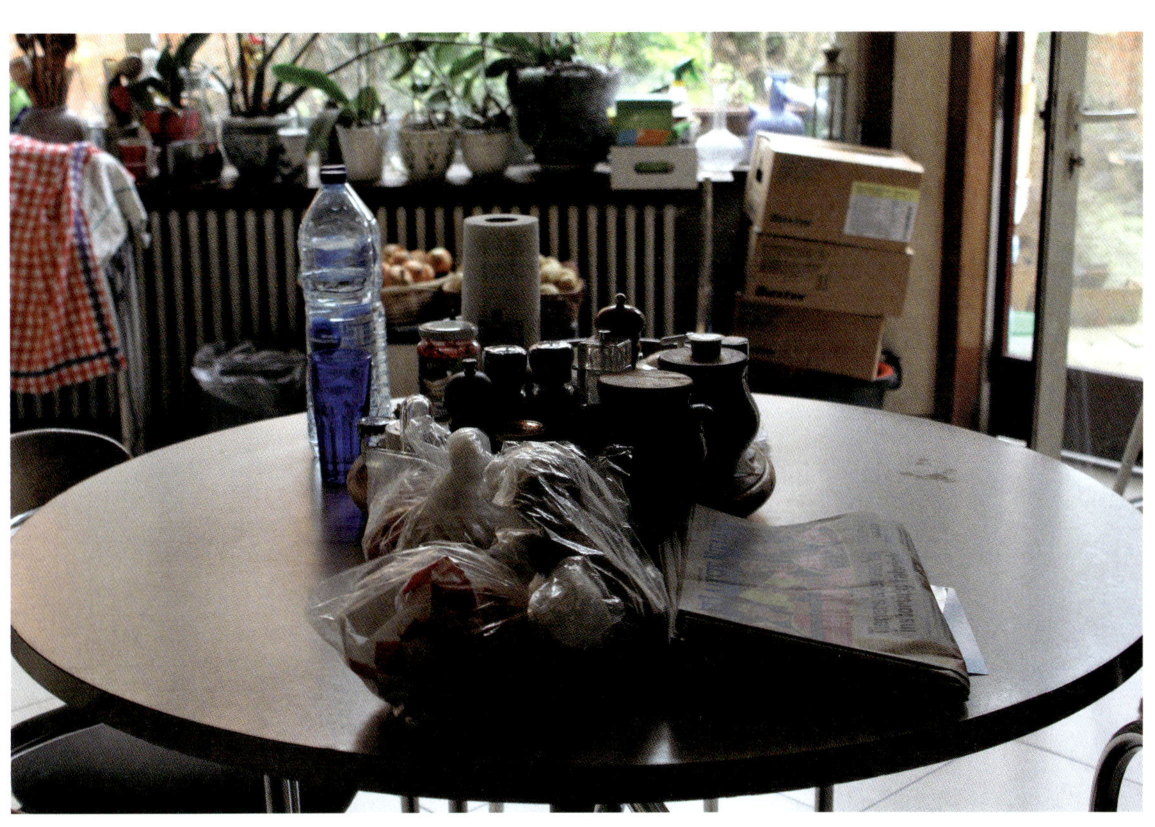

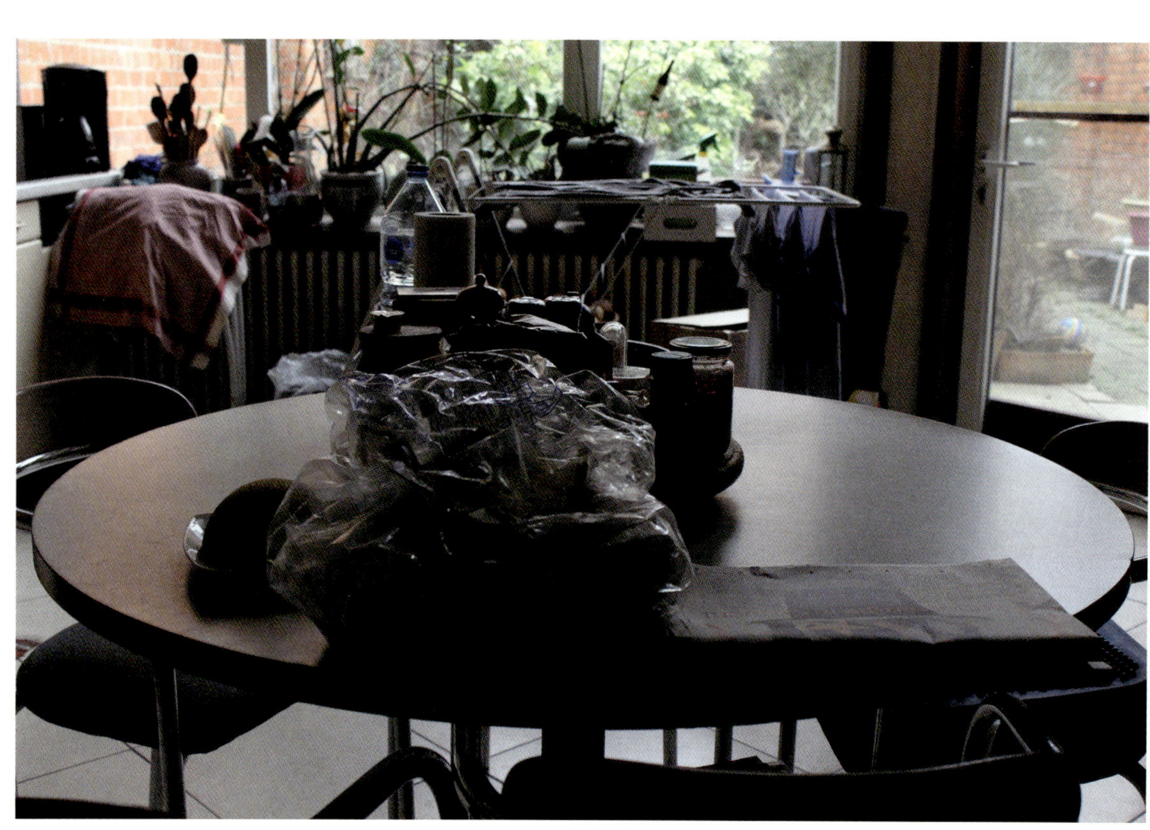

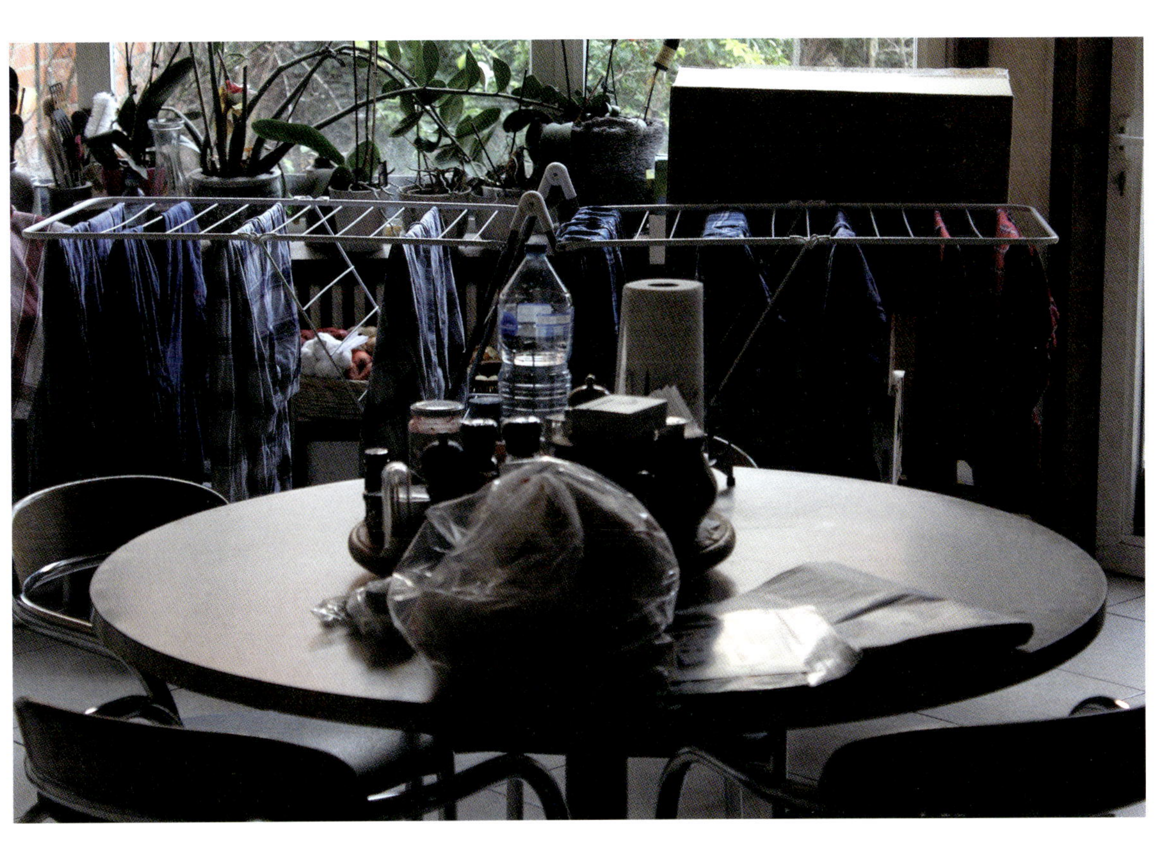

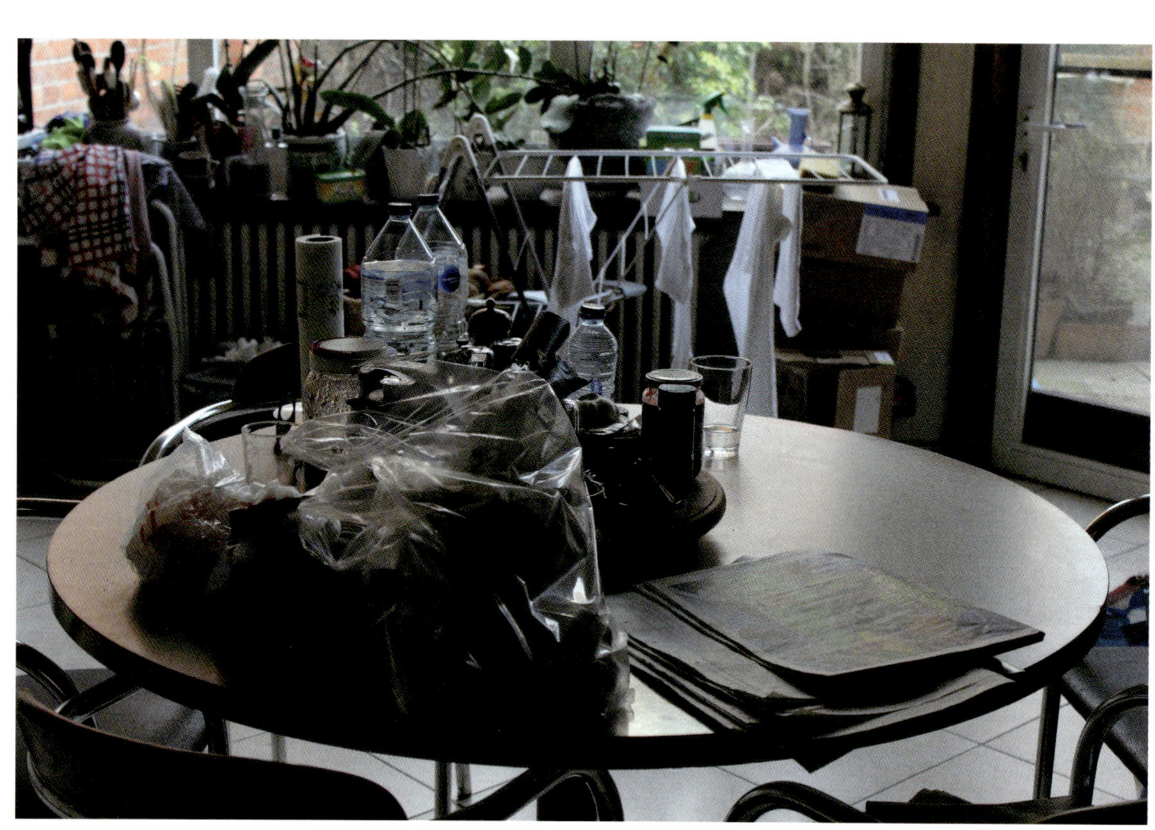

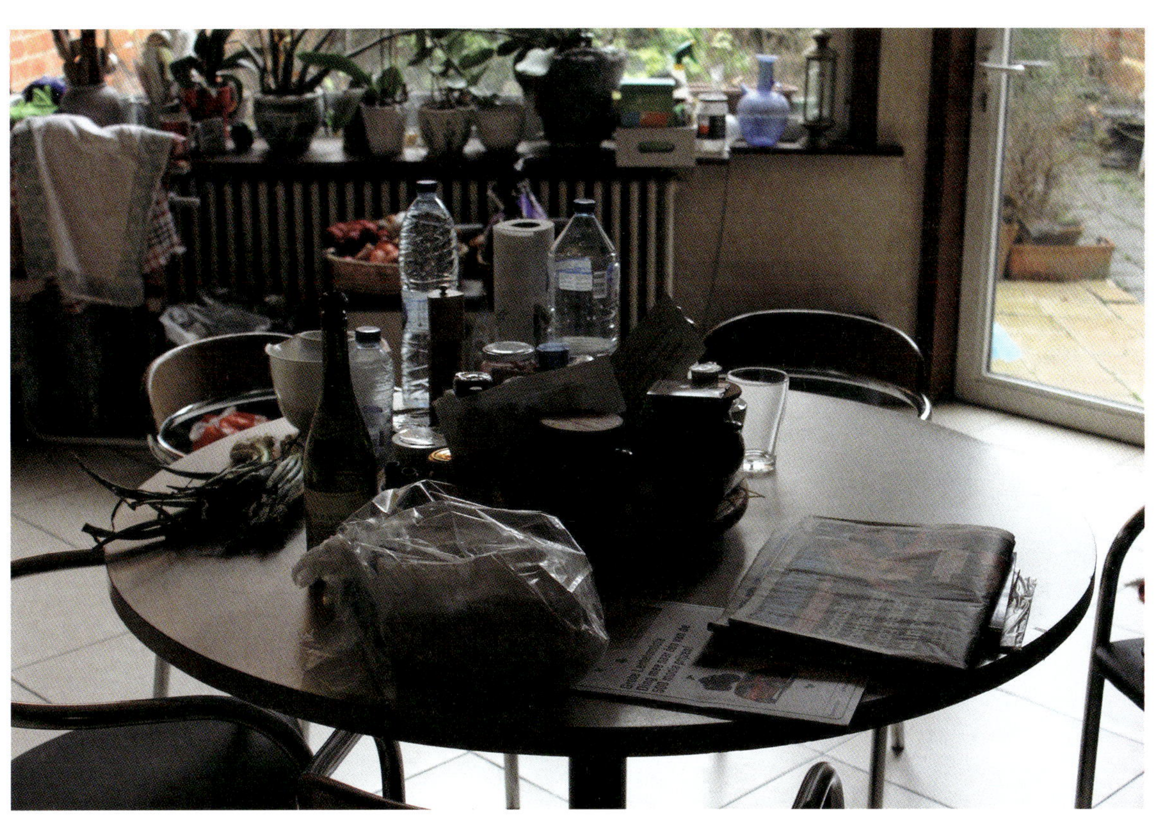

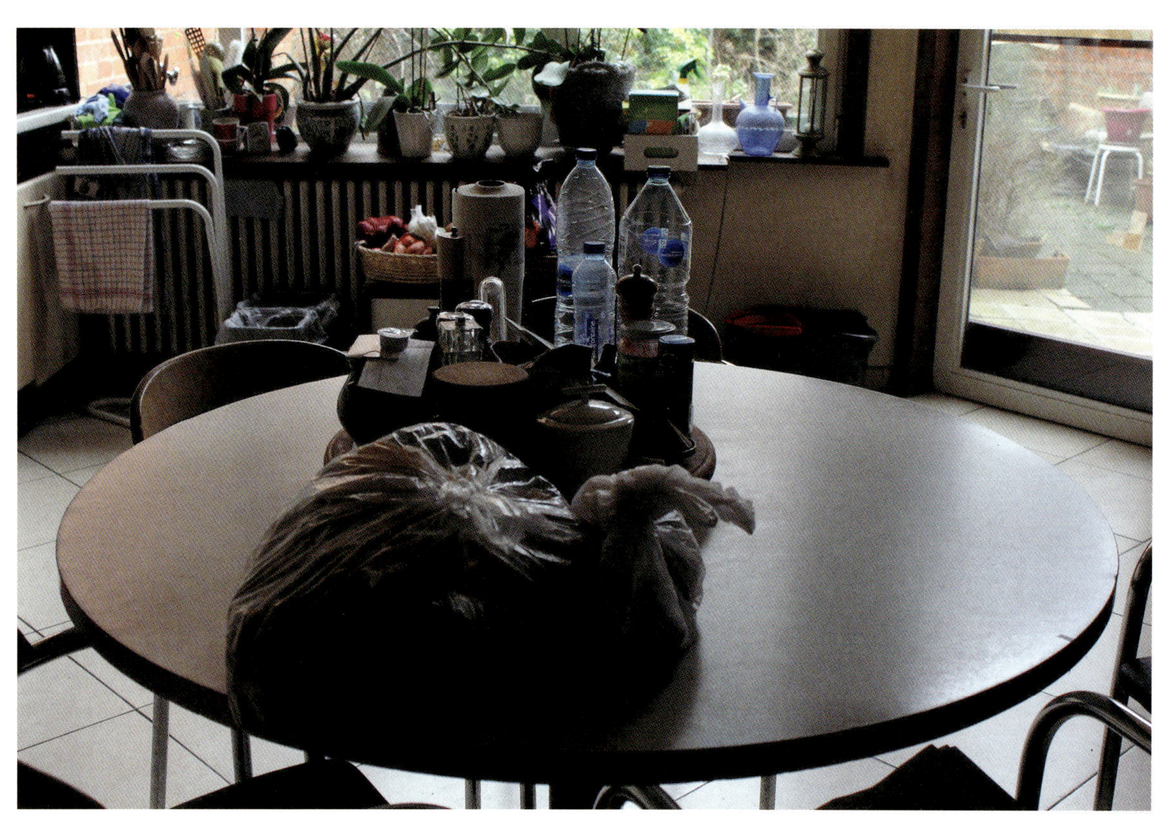

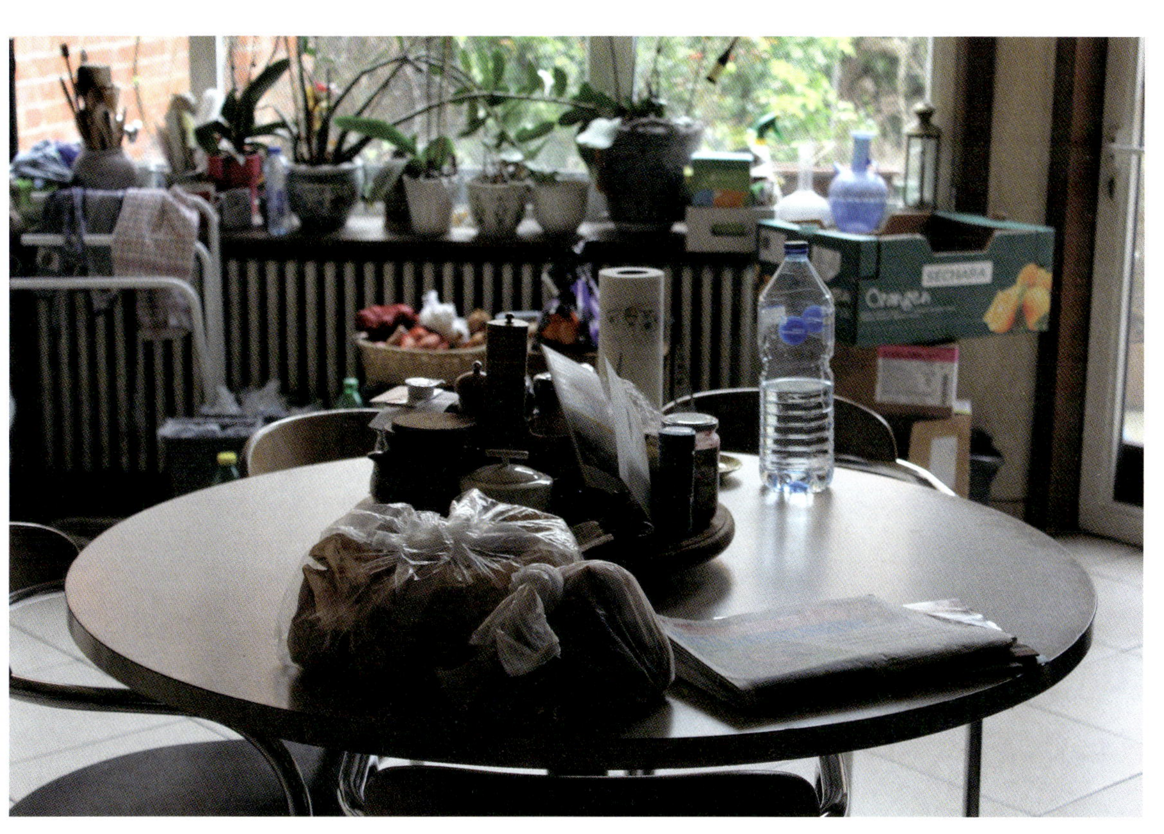

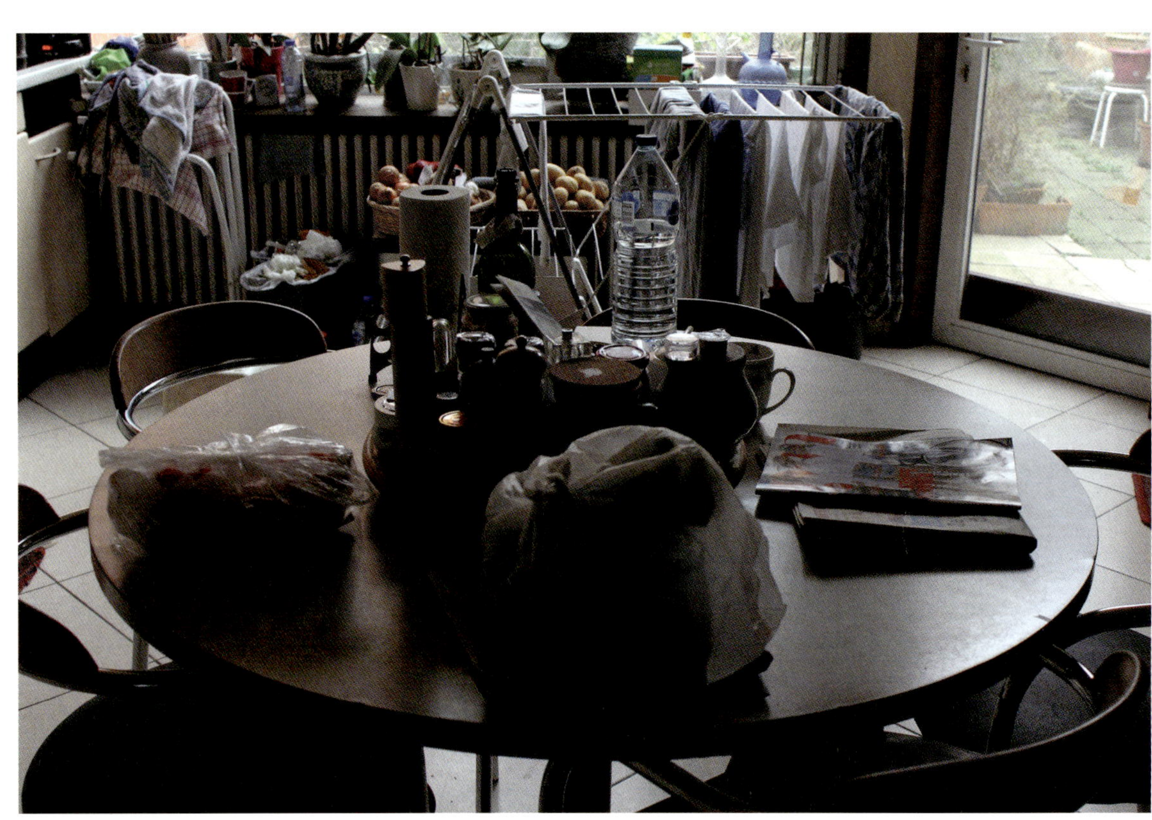

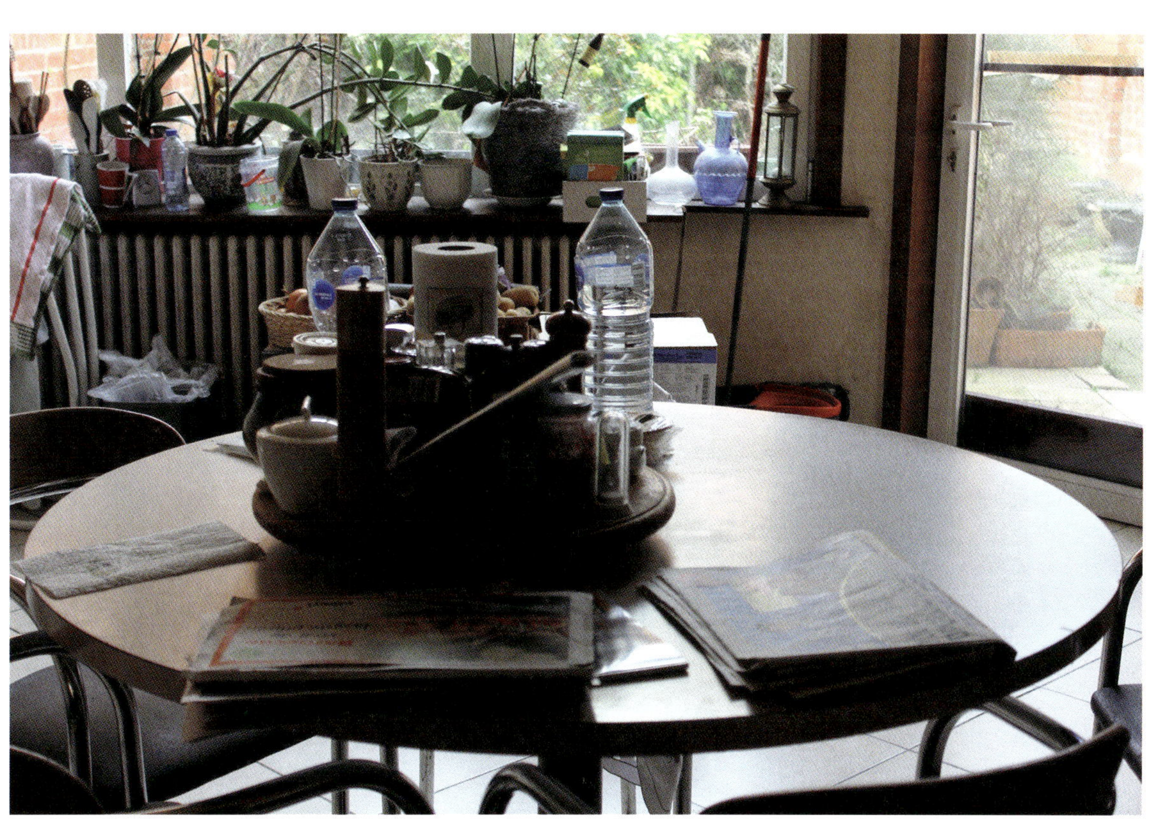

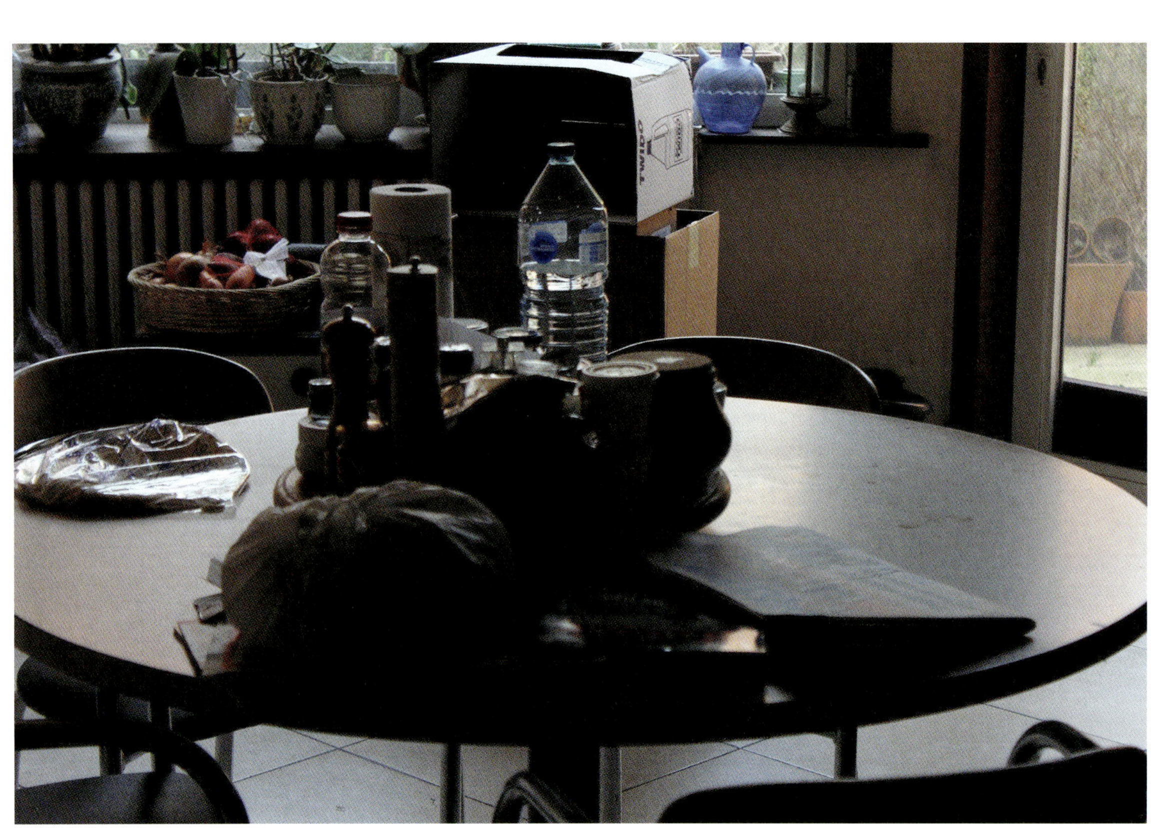

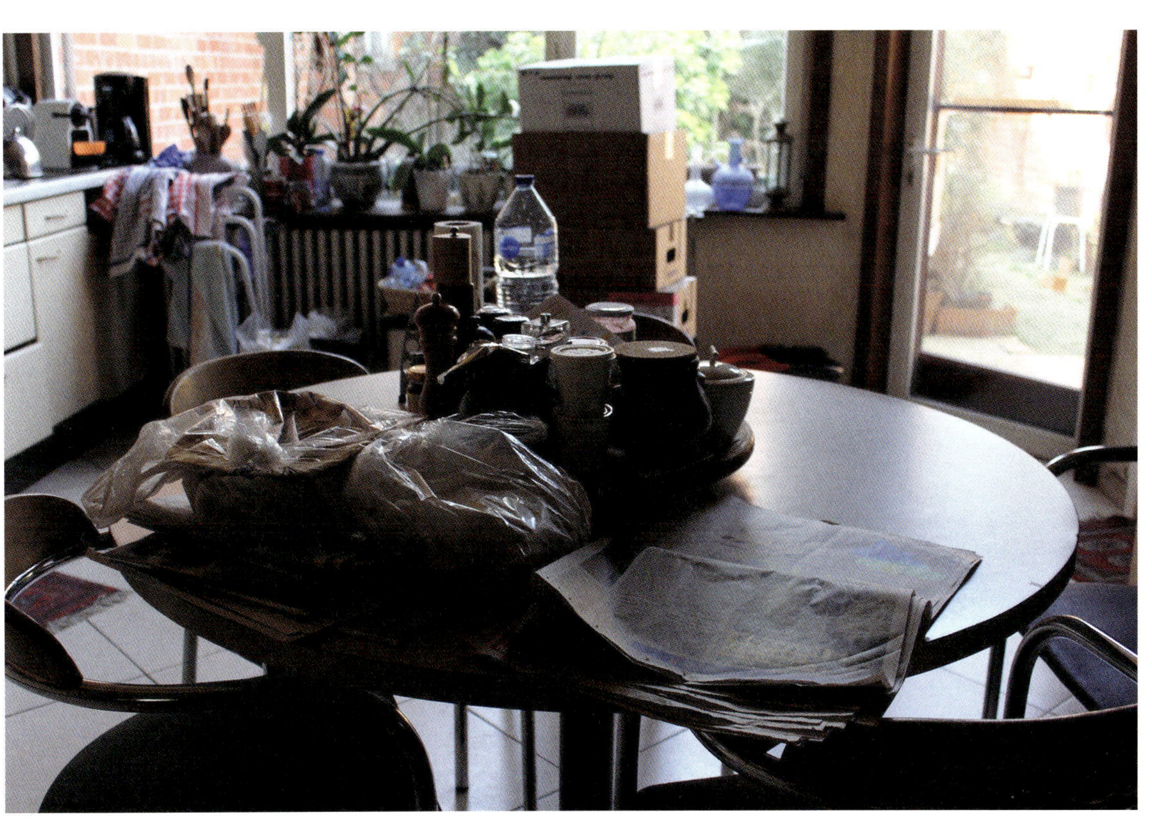

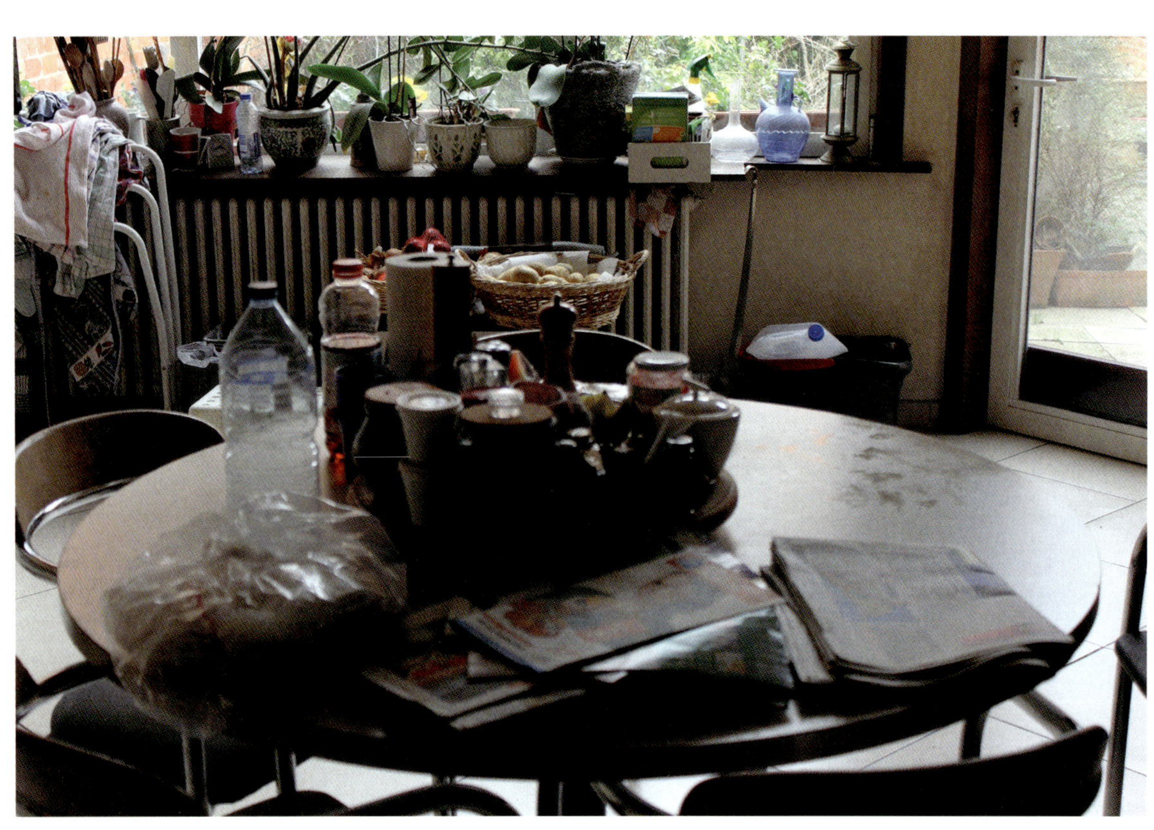

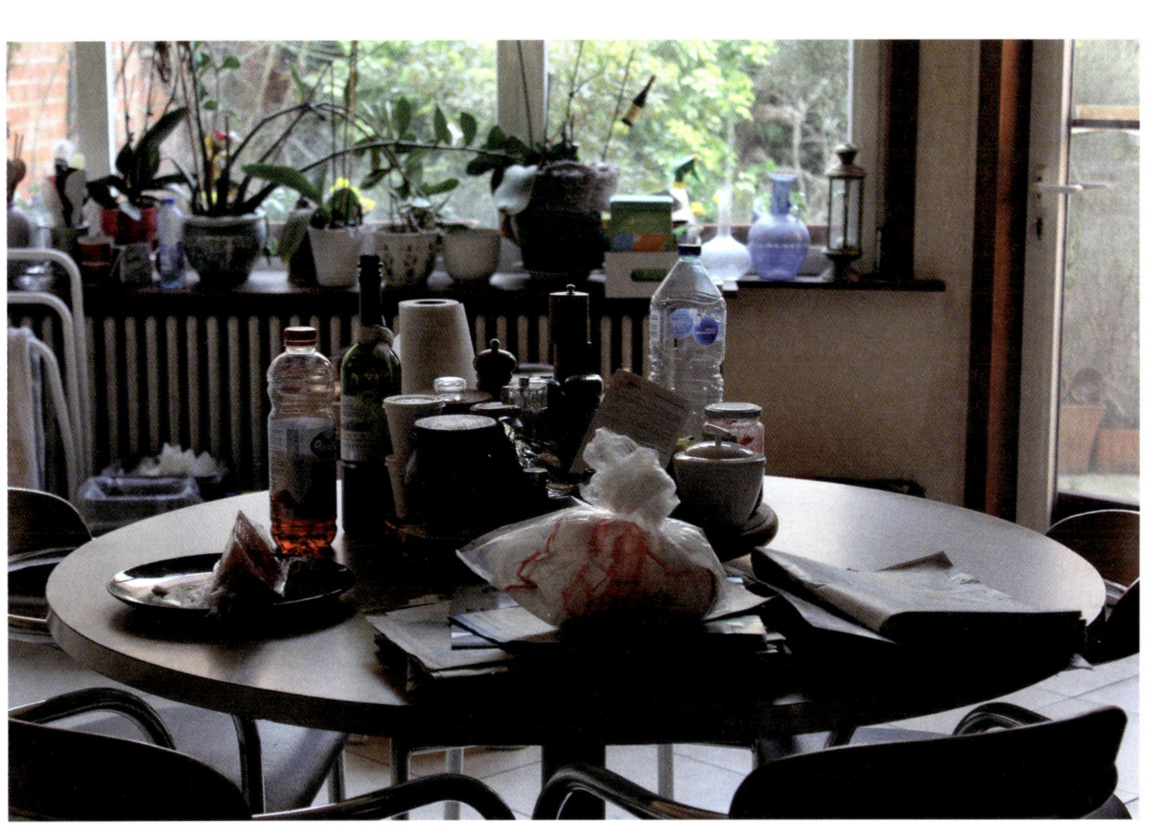

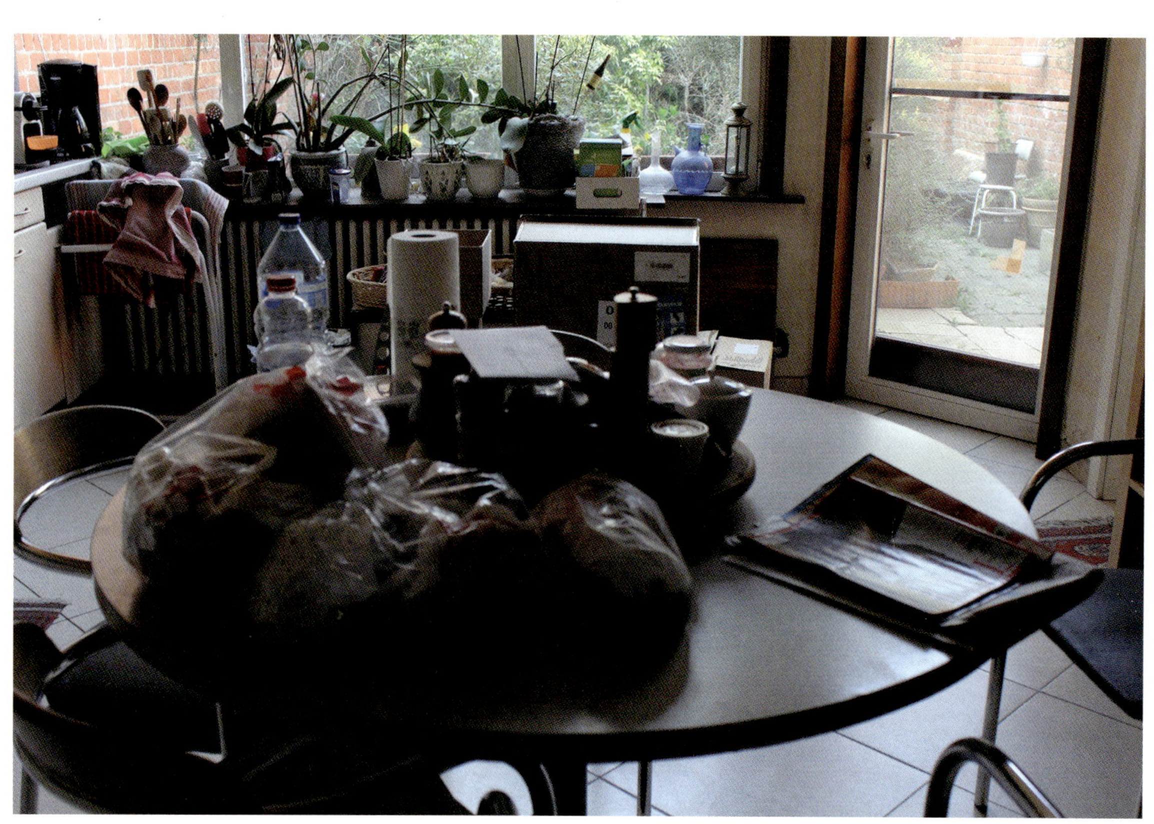

for Laurice Karaguezian

This seeking for my home...
was my affliction (Heimsuchung)...
Where is — my home?
I ask and seek and have sought for it;
I have not found it.

Friedrich Nietzsche, *Also sprach Zarathustra*,
in Walter Benjamin, 'Paris, Capital of the
Nineteenth Century (Exposé of 1939)'

Artist book published on the occasion of Mekhitar Garabedian's solo show

UN BEL ÉTÉ QUAND MÊME

24 June – 29 September 2015, BOZAR, Centre for Fine Arts, Brussels
Supported by Albert Baronian, Nathalie Oghlian & Peter Hrechdakian

It is with good reason that we invited Mekhitar Garabedian to take part in our Antichambres programme in this symbolic year of 2015. It marks the 100th commemoration of the Armenian genocide, from which his grandparents fled.

Mekhitar Garabedian is a Belgian-Syrian artist of Armenian descent who gives language form by employing it as image and vice versa: the text is the image and the image is the text. His work is influenced by the thinking of such artists as Jean-Luc Godard and Marcel Broodthaers. Garabedian is a discrete person, whose artistic work can in a sense be compared to silent films. His art brings across a charming 'something' that connects on different levels. He rejects spectacular visual culture, structuring instead the obscured memories of an intangible history and rearranging them within the realm of poetic memory. Mikhail Bakhtin wrote that 'language may remember its life only in poetic contexts.' We quote Morson & Emerson on Bakhtin, saying, 'that his [the novelist's] language is one of doubts, not because he uses language to express doubts, but because he doubts his own language. By contrast, poetic language is not doubted even when it expresses doubt.' If we lose language, we lose knowledge about the world in which we live. When we preserve language, we can use it for (migrating) stories and texts. Mekhitar Garabedian's artistic practice concentrates on linguistic identity and the quintessence of the diaspora. In the light of ever-increasing waves of migration and the questions that diasporas pose, his work, as it unites several layers of identity and meaning in this unique language of images and forms, is more relevant and more important than ever before.

We are exceptionally pleased to present this two-part artist's book. Both installations, *Table, Gentbrugge (Kitchen)* and *Table, Gentbrugge (Living Room)*, are on view in the exhibition.

Our thanks are extended to Céline Butaye, who knows as no other how to translate Garabedian's work to book form, to Christel Tsilibaris, Anne Judong and Gunther De Wit for the coordination of the exhibition and the book, respectively, and we are highly appreciative of the support that Albert Baronian has given the project. This is also true for Nathalie Oghlian and Peter Hrechdakian.

Last but not least, we are greatly indebted to the artist for so generously accepting our invitation.

SOPHIE LAUWERS

HEAD OF EXHIBITIONS

PAUL DUJARDIN

DIRECTOR GENERAL AND ARTISTIC DIRECTOR

BOZAR, CENTRE FOR FINE ARTS, BRUSSELS

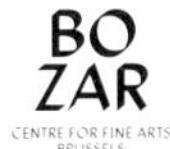

EXHIBITION

CHIEF EXECUTIVE OFFICER & ARTISTIC DIRECTOR Paul Dujardin **HEAD OF EXHIBITIONS** Sophie Lauwers **HEAD OF PRODUCTION** Evelyne Hinque **EXHIBITION COORDINATORS** Anne Judong, Christel Tsilibaris **BOZAR EXPO TEAM** Axelle Ancion, Helena Bussers, Francis Carpentier, Mieke De Bock, Christophe De Jaeger, Rocío del Casar Ximénez, Gunther De Wit, Ann Flas, Ann Geeraerts, Anne Judong, Vera Kotaji, Kathleen Louw, Alberta Sessa, Christel Tsilibaris, Dieter Van den Storm **TECHNICAL COORDINATOR** Isabelle Speybrouck **ART HANDLING & INSTALLATION** BOZAR art handlers

DIRECTION COMMITTEE & MANAGEMENT

CHIEF EXECUTIVE OFFICER & ARTISTIC DIRECTOR Paul Dujardin **DIRECTOR OF ARTISTIC POLICY** Adinda Van Geystelen **DIRECTOR OF OPERATIONS** Albert Wastiaux **DIRECTOR OF FINANCES** Jérémie Leroy **HEAD OF EXHIBITIONS** Sophie Lauwers **HEAD OF MUSIC** Ulrich Hauschild **HEAD OF CINEMA** Juliette Duret **DIRECTOR OF MARKETING, COMMUNICATION & SALES** Filip Stuer **DIRECTOR OF TECHNICS, IT, INVESTMENTS, SAFETY AND SECURITY** Stéphane Vanreppelen **DIRECTOR OF PRODUCTION & PLANNING** Jean-François D'hondt **DIRECTOR OF GENERAL ADMINISTRATION** Didier Verboomen **DIRECTOR OF HUMAN RESOURCES** Marleen Spileers

PUBLICATION

PUBLISHER BOZAR BOOKS **CO-PUBLISHER & DISTRIBUTION** MER. Paper Kunsthalle, Ghent **PUBLICATION COORDINATOR** Gunther De Wit **AUTHORS** Liene Aerts, Pieter Van Bogaert **TRANSLATOR** Mari Shields **BOOK DESIGN** Céline Butaye **PRINTED BY** Graphius, Ghent

PHOTO CREDITS

all photos by Mekhitar Garabedian
courtesy the artist and Albert Baronian Gallery

Mekhitar Garabedian is affiliated to the Royal Academy of Fine Arts, University College Ghent since 2009, where he is working on a PhD in the visual arts.

© 2015 BOZAR, Centre for Fine Arts, Brussels, the artist, and all authors

ISBN 9789074816465
D/2015/2634/6

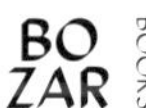  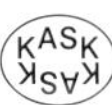 HoGent